The Historic Houses of Edinburgh

The Historic Houses of Edinburgh

JOYCE M. WALLACE

SECOND EDITION

JOHN DONALD PUBLISHERS LTD
EDINBURGH

© Joyce M. Wallace 1998

First published 1987
Second edition 1998

All rights reserved.
No part of this publication may be reproduced
in any form or by any means without
the prior permission of the publishers
John Donald Publishers Limited,
73, Logie Green Road, Edinburgh, EH7 4HF.

ISBN 0 85976 503 2

British Library Cataloguing in Publication Data.

A catalogue record for this book is available
from the British Library.

The illustrations are from photographs by the author.

Typesetting by WestKey Limited, Falmouth, Cornwall
Printed and bound in Great Britain by Bell & Bain Ltd., Glasgow

Contents

To Lawrie Pentland (Mrs I. L. Glass)
for our shared interest in historic Edinburgh

Up there in the centre of Edinburgh . . .
the houses bulge outwards on flimsy
brackets . . . a gable and a few
crowsteps are printed on the sky . . .
here you find a great old mansion still
erect . . . come suddenly on a corner
and see . . . woods and villas and a
blue arm of the sea . . . the road begins
to scale . . . the Pentlands . . . this is
Swanston and consists of a few cottages
on a green beside a burn.

R.L. Stevenson

OTHER BOOKS BY JOYCE M. WALLACE
PUBLISHED BY JOHN DONALD LTD.

Canonmills and Inverleith
Traditions of Trinity and Leith
Further Traditions of Trinity and Leith

Preface to the Second Edition

It is now eleven years since the first publication of this book and in that time changes have, inevitably, taken place in the City of Edinburgh. In addition, other houses of historic interest, lurking unnoticed during earlier research, have been discovered and a few have, sadly, disappeared during these years as a consequence of which Parson's Green House, Denham Green House, the house with the scrolled skewputts in Inglis Green Road, The Cedars at Corstorphine, Windlestrawlee farm cottage beside Ferry Road, Drylaw Mains Farmhouse used as a police station in Ferry Road (demolished and replaced by the large, modern Drylaw Police Station) and Upper Braid have now been deleted.

The opportunity has also been taken to correct errors, update the previous information and rewrite the text where this has been considered appropriate for incorporation of new material or clarity of presentation.

Edinburgh 1998
J.M.W.

Acknowledgements

Grateful acknowledgment is made to the staff of the Edinburgh Room at the Edinburgh Central Public Library for untiring assistance in the searching of records, to Dr A.G.H. Macpherson for permission to photograph Laverockdale House, to Mr Charles Drysdale for permission to photograph Liberton Tower Mains, to Sir John Crofton for help in identifying the house called The Bush in Spylaw Bank Road, to Elizabeth Cumming, formerly Keeper of Edinburgh City Art Collection, for information relating to Phoebe Traquair of The Bush, and to Strathearn Advertising Ltd. for information relating to Silvermills House.

Preface to the First Edition

Even in the 18th century Edinburgh was noted for the large number of mansions and country houses within it and in its close vicinity. In the preparation of this book an attempt has been made to give a short but sufficiently explanatory history and description of the many houses which, either in whole or in part, still remain to lend beauty, variety and interest to the environment. All are within the city limits defined by the Edinburgh Boundaries Extension Act of 1920, and the criterion for inclusion has been the age, history, architectural merit or unusual nature of the building and, of course, the fame or other interesting characteristics of the succeeding occupants. In Part II in particular, dealing with the Georgian New Town, where every house could in truth be said to meet at least one of these requirements, streets are discussed as well as their individual houses and those who lived in them. Small houses, cottages and lodges have been included, and houses of minor interest (printed in capital letters) have been inserted under the heading of the geographically nearest house of greater significance.

Although it is not claimed that this is a comprehensive review of all the historic houses within the City of Edinburgh (one of the most fascinating aspects of its study is its seeming inexhaustibility), every effort has been made towards the achieving of that aim.

Edinburgh   J.M.W.
1986

Part I
The Old Town

The origins of the ancient city of Edinburgh are remote – too remote to have been chronicled, too remote for chronicles to have survived throughout its long and turbulent history – but it can be said with some degree of certainty that the site of its first occupation was the Castle rock and that it first existed as a primitive hill fort at some time before the arrival of the Roman legions in the First Century A.D. Recent excavation work to cut a tunnel for traffic through the rock has, in fact, pushed the date of occupation at least as far back as 500 B.C.

As castle and town developed, so also did an ecclesiastical foundation, the Abbey of Holyrood, at the lower end of the volcanic ridge which was to define the city's cragbound limits till after the middle of the 18th century. On the crest of the ridge a long street linking the town and the abbey eventually evolved – a long street with wynds and closes that ran steeply down its rocky flanks to north and south – a long street of lands, or tenements, that grew higher and ever higher because they could not spread outwards – a long street of houses, most of which, if built before the Reformation, would have been roofed with thatch. Those which stand today on the old foundations give some idea of what the Auld Toun looked like before its straitened boundaries were broken through and the worn-out habitations left to decay and moulder into slums. From that state they have been revived, reinvigorated, reproduced or replaced in more recent years and tell their story in stone to all who walk among them down the ancient way.

Acheson House

Acheson House stands, on the east side of Bakehouse Close on the south side of the Canongate in Old Edinburgh's Royal Mile. The

The crowstepped gable and weathered stonework of 17th century Acheson House.

town house of Sir Archibald Acheson, Bart., of Glencairnie, a Secretary of State for Scotland under Charles I by whom he was knighted, it was built by him in 1633. His initials and those of his wife, Dame Margaret Hamilton, appear in the pediment above the narrow, moulded doorway of the house, together with the date of building. Over the initials curves a scroll bearing the motto *Vigilantibus* and at the top is a cock standing on a trumpet.

The ashlar-built mansion is ornamented by stringcourses and dormer windows with finialled pediments. This old residence was well restored by the fourth Marquis of Bute in 1937, and oyster shells, at one time believed to ward off evil spirits, can still be seen embedded in its street-facing gable wall.

Bailie Macmorran's House

B uilt in the 16th century, Bailie Macmorran's House is situated behind the south side of the Lawnmarket within an inner courtyard entered from Riddle's Close which John Geddie has praised as 'one of the best preserved and most interesting of the Old Edinburgh alleys.'

John Macmorran, a wealthy merchant and city magistrate, allowed his fine house to be used on occasion as a place of civic entertainment, but it was also the place from which he went unsuspectingly to a tragic death at the hands of rebellious schoolboys. The reputation of the famous High School of Edinburgh was being seriously jeopardised by the behaviour of its scholars in the late 1590s, but the events which took place there when an expected holiday had been denied to the pupils on one occasion were to lead their subdued and penitent perpetrators to mend their ways. They decided to wreak revenge for their deprivation and, arming themselves with swords and pistols, set off at midnight for the school to set 'all authority at defiance', as James Grant describes it. Other attempted remedies having been tried without success, Bailie Macmorran and some city officers entered the school yard. The magistrate ordered the officers to break down the door, and they were about to enter the building when a shot fired from one of the windows hit the bailie on his forehead, killing him instantly. Shocked into panic by the consequences of their revolt, some tried to escape while others submitted and, including William Sinclair, a son of Chancellor Sinclair of Caithness, who had fired the shot, were taken into custody and put in jail. Lord Sinclair, however, had too much influence in high places for his son to pay the price of his misdeeds, and in the end no punishment was imposed on any of the participants. His act of violence did not lie so heavily on William Sinclair's conscience as to prevent his marriage in due time and his acceptance of the title of Sir William Sinclair of Mey in 1631, as a result of which he became the progenitor of the Earls of Caithness.

Shortly after the sad demise of Bailie Macmorran his house was the scene of a lavish banquet given by the Town Council of Edinburgh in honour of the visiting Duke of Holstein, a brother of Anne of Denmark, the wife of James VI who was also present.

The house remained in the Macmorran family for several generations before it passed to Sir John Clerk of Penicuik who sold it to a senator of the College of Justice, Sir Roderick Mackenzie of Preston Hall. At the end of the 19th century Pattrick Geddes, as part of his rehabilitation work in the Royal Mile, had the old building altered and restored for the University of Edinburgh.

With its irregular stringcourses, acutely pointed gable pediments and doorways flanked by finialled pilasters, the prevailing atmosphere is that of the old Scots vernacular tradition, and the house is ornamented within by elaborate plaster ceilings as well as by panelling of the early 18th century and a painted ceiling dating from the Geddes restoration. A wooden windowframe with carved ornament from Bailie Macmorran's House is preserved in Huntly House Museum.

Boswell's Court

Situated in Castlehill, the first section of the Royal Mile immediately below the Castle Esplanade, is the five-storey tenement, dating from the early 1600s with pedimented dormer windows and a crowstepped gable called after Dr Boswell, an uncle of the more famous James, the biographer of Dr Samuel Johnson, who lived here from the end of the 17th century.

Over the moulded entrance doorway are the now somewhat obliterated words O. LORD. IN. THE. IS. AL. MI. TRAIST., one of several scriptural inscriptions which it was common practice to place on old Scottish dwellinghouses of that period.

Brodie's Close

Like Riddle's Close, Brodie's Close lies on the south side of the Lawnmarket. Although his house no longer survives, it was in this close that, along with his father who was also a wright, the notorious Deacon William Brodie lived as respected citizen, skilled and reputable cabinet-maker and Deacon of Wrights and Masons, and as a conscientious member of the Edinburgh Town Council in the 1780s. This supposedly upright character did not, however, scruple to turn daring criminal at night, gaining entrance to his victims' shops and houses by unlocking them with duplicate keys which he himself had previously made. A long series of unsolved burglaries was to terrorise the Old Town before his career was brought to a conclusion when he was hanged on a gibbet which he himself had only recently improved! His lantern and substitute keys have been preserved for posterity.

Brodie's Close can be assigned to the 17th century but it and other closes on the south side of the Lawnmarket were truncated by the building of Victoria Terrace in the 19th century. As John Geddie wryly remarks, 'it is the world's way that earlier and worthier possessors and name-fathers of this Lawnmarket block – the learned and generous Littles of Craigmillar, who were founders of the University and its library – should be forgotten, and the infamous William Brodie held in perpetual remembrance.' He lies with his betters in the burial ground of the former Buccleuch Parish Church, then known as St. Cuthbert's Chapel of Ease.

Byres Close – Bishop Bothwell's House

A most unusual building, dating from the 17th century, projects northwards on the west side of Advocates Close in the High Street. It is said to have belonged to Adam Bothwell, Bishop of Orkney and Commendator of Holyrood, who performed the Protestant marriage ceremony for Mary, Queen of Scots, and her third husband, the Earl of Bothwell, in 1567. The tall, narrow structure terminates in a three-sided 'apsidal' curve towards the north, the three upper windows being surmounted by semicircular pediments containing Latin inscriptions. Chambers in his *Traditions of Edinburgh* refers to the house 'on top of which is a bartisan or flat roof, faced with three lettered stones.' He cannot, he says, confirm the tradition that Oliver Cromwell 'used to come out and sit here to view his navy on the Forth.' It was, however, not impossible as Cromwell 'is said to have had his guardhouse in the neighbouring alley.' Indeed, Cromwell's connection would seem to be more probable than Bishop Bothwell's as the Bishop died at the end of the 16th century, the house being built about thirty years thereafter.

Byres Close - an unusual building, said to have belonged to Bishop Bothwell, in the High Street.

External restoration in 1977 revealed a row of six earthenware pots set into the stonework of the house at a height of about forty feet. The pots, with their open ends to the outside, are probably acoustic jars which were frequently placed in the fabric of buildings to improve the quality of sound when it was intended that musical instruments would be played, and are consequently sometimes found in churches. The holes can be clearly seen from ground level.

Byres Close takes its name from the Edinburgh merchant, John Byres of Coates, whose townhouse was located here, and Advocates Close from Sir James Stewart of Goodtrees, Lord Advocate in the late 17th and early 18th centuries.

Cadell House

Near Panmure House (q.v.) in the Canongate is the 18th century Cadell House. This well-proportioned and attractive building has suffered badly from reconstruction and has now been flatted for 20th century occupation. It is said to have belonged to the iron-milling Cadell family of Cramond (see Cramond House).

Cannonball House

Cannonball House beside the Castle Esplanade. A cannonball is embedded in the wall on the left but is not visible here.

Overlooking Castle Wynd, the steps which lead down to Johnston Terrace, and entered from Castlehill, is Cannonball House. The date on a dormer window pediment, in lieu of a marriage lintel, is 1630, and the initials AM-MN refer to the Edinburgh merchant Alexander Mure (he was a furrier) and his wife Margaret Neillans who settled here in that year. The eponymous cannonball is said to have been fired from the Castle during the period following Prince Charles Edward Stuart's arrival in the capital in 1745 and to have become embedded in the wall, but the more generally accepted explanation is that it marks the height from which the city's first water supply was brought to the reservoir opposite the house by gravitational descent from Comiston Springs in 1676. The water was then carried down in pipes to the public wells in the Royal Mile.

A country-style 18th century house in the Royal Mile which is now the Canongate Manse.

Enlarged during the 18th century, Cannonball House was again altered just before the First World War and incorporated into Castlehill School.

Canongate Manse

In the days when the town of Edinburgh stopped at the Netherbow Port, the Canongate – the road to the Abbey – was a fashionable area where the landed nobles of Scotland chose to build their townhouses. On the north side, a short distance below Canongate Church, stands the plain, two-storeyed, harled building with projecting wings on either side which in course of time became the Canongate Manse.

It stands back within Reid's Court which the late Ian G. Lindsay pointed out as being 'marked on old maps as Reid's Coach Yard.' It was built in the first half of the 18th century and the same writer considered it to have 'more the appearance of a farm-house than a town mansion.' In 1958 it was restored by Ian G. Lindsay & Partners.

RUSSELL HOUSE, a student residence, is on the east side of Reid's Court.

Chessel's Court

Chessel's Court (called after Archibald Chessel, a carpenter and builder) on the south side of the Canongate had the good fortune to be restored by Robert Hurd & Partners in the 1960s. The main, central block contains flats of mid-18th century vintage and, with its stair-tower and high chimney gable, contrasts the traditional Scottish architectural style with the symmetrical door and window spacing which characterises the later Georgian houses of the New Town.

It was here, in a part of the building used as the Excise Office, that Deacon Brodie committed his ultimate burglary. Aware that he had been seen, he fled to Leith and from there to Amsterdam but, pursued and brought back to Edinburgh to stand trial, he was hanged in 1788 (see Brodie's Close).

Crocket's Land

The West Bow was once the south-west entrance to the Old Town. It linked the Grassmarket and the Lawnmarket and had a high and ancient house, now swept away, at the top and the Bowfoot Well, which is still there, at the foot. The upper portion of the Bow, apart from a short section known as the Upper Bow, was destroyed when George IV Bridge and Victoria Street and Terrace were built in the 1830s. The lower Bow is now joined on to Victoria Street which runs to meet it from George IV Bridge, its name commemorating the famous visit of that monarch in 1822.

Several old and remarkable buildings remain in what is left of the West Bow, Crocket's Land being of especial interest. It dates from the late 17th century and, as usual, takes its name from its builder, Thomas Crocket of Johnstounburn, who was probably a merchant. The high, narrow house of four floors has an attic storey in a curving gable where attractive features above the windows and beneath the tall, central chimney stack are the two oval pigeon holes with nesting places for the birds in the gable.

Crocket's Land was some years ago given a new lease of life. Partitioning sub-dividing the old dwelling into small flats was removed and, during repairs to wood panelling in the first-floor dining-room, a secret cupboard was revealed behind a panel which had been hinged to form an opening. Another panel also opened and was found to give access to the adjoining room. There are two rooms on each floor, and the panelling and other Georgian features were put in in 1735, a time of Jacobite intrigue, which may account for the inclusion of concealed openings and hiding places. The dining-room extends across the front of the building and has an arched corner recess, a panelled corner cupboard, an open fireplace and a wooden cornice. Panelling along the length of one wall in one of the two bedrooms on the fourth floor conceals a large storage area behind, and this room also has a corner cupboard.

An Old Town house of great character and interest, the preservation and restoration of Crocket's Land have created a unique link with a vanished way of life in the old city.

Croft-an-Righ

The turreted, 16th century townhouse of the Earls of Airth – its name meaning King's Croft or King's Field and recalled by Scott in *Chronicles of the Canongate* – stands eastward of the Palace of Holyroodhouse, off Abbeyhill, most of the building dating from the following century. The Regent Morton is said to have lived here but it is unlikely that the little mansion of Croft-an-Righ was there in his day.

Conical roofs surmount the angle turrets of this most attractive rubble-built survivor from a period when Scotland's history was in

Croft-an-Righ – a charming, mainly 17th-century house near Holyrood Palace which has been restored by Historic Scotland.

the making, and inside there is a good 17th century plaster ceiling, elaborately carved, at first-floor level.

In its secluded backwater it has now been restored as their regional office by Historic Scotland, having previously been divided into two flats for Palace gardeners.

Cross House

A pproached from New Skinners Close off the east side of Black-friars Street is the rubble-built, four-storeyed Cross House with

The Cross House, behind Blackfriars street, where Dr Guthrie's original ragged school was located.

a long wing stretching back to Blackfriars Street on the south side. A semi-octagonal tower in the re-entrant angle contains the stair, and pedimented dormer windows, a moulded doorway and an old street lamp adorn the frontage.

The building was originally entered through a close on the south side of the High Street, and dates from the mid-17th century but is largely of the early 18th when its adaptation as the Skinners' Hall probably took place.

It was in Cross House that Dr Thomas Guthrie began his famous and highly successful 'ragged school' experiment when an additional wing was added about the middle of the 19th century. In 1982 the extended house was developed as residential accommodation by the Edinburgh City Architect's Department.

Edinburgh Castle

The origins of Edinburgh Castle are lost in antiquity. The historical record begins in the 11th century when Malcolm III and Queen Margaret chose to live within it, the Saxon queen adorning the rude Canmore apartments with luxuries until then unknown in Scotland, but no trace of the buildings of that early period now remains.

Occupied by the forces of Henry II of England in 1174, the Castle was returned to Scotland as a dowry to his English queen on the marriage of William the Lion; it was the safe haven for Alexander III, married at the age of ten to Margaret, the little daughter of Henry III, during their minority; and it was again in English hands after its surrender to Edward I from 1296–1313.

The Scottish kings continued to use the Castle as their principal place of residence and it sheltered, either as refuge or as prison, the early child-kings of the House of Stewart. It was the fourth James, however, who ended its status as a royal house when he commenced the building of a palace beside the Abbey of Holyrood at the other extremity of the Royal Mile (see Holyrood Palace). But James VI was born there in the little room which can still be visited, while more alarms and excursions engulfed the Castle during the troubles that followed the reign of his mother, Mary Queen of Scots.

The much-altered Palace or King's Lodging, dating from the 15th century, and the Great Hall built by James IV on the south side of

Edinburgh Castle and the Ross Fountain from the north-west.

Palace Yard also still remain, as do the ruins of the Wellhouse Tower, the source of water for the Castle, below the Castle rock in Princes Street Gardens.

The fortress was once more besieged and captured in the mid-17th century by Cromwell's army, but the guns on the rock were fired for peaceful purposes to mark the Restoration of Charles II and its final freedom from English occupation. The last siege was in 1688 when James VII and II was exiled and William and Mary commenced their reign, and the turbulent history of the ancient stronghold was finally brought to an end after the city was bombarded by the Castle cannon when Bonnie Prince Charlie and his Highlanders entered Edinburgh in 1745.

The French prisoners captured during the Napoleonic Wars were incarcerated in the vaulted casemates beneath the Great Hall, but it is on record that 'they did not complain of their treatment.' They were sent back to France in 1795 and the Castle became, and has since remained, a military garrison. But long before that its day as a house of kings had been brought to an end.

Edinburgh Castle Governor's House

Situated near the New Barracks at Edinburgh Castle, at a lower level than Palace Yard (now known as Crown Square) is the Governor's house. Dating from 1742, this attractive building has two main storeys, an attic storey and a double basement across which access is obtained through the projecting portico. The two plain lower wings were originally separate houses and the central block, which was the Governor's residence, is distinguished by heavily emphasised gable crowsteps and five pedimented dormer windows behind a parapet at the roofline. The separate houses in the wings were originally occupied by the master gunner and the storekeeper. The whole building is now used as an Officers' Mess.

Gladstone's Land

Ian G. Lindsay called Gladstone's Land one of the finest houses in Edinburgh. This tall, somewhat narrow building on an originally restricted site rises up through six storeys and terminates in two pointed gables of unequal size. It is entered from the north side of the Lawnmarket where curving forestairs jut out onto the pavement immediately westward of an arcaded ground-floor frontage consisting of two round-headed arches. These were rediscovered during restoration work carried out after the Land was purchased in 1934 by The National Trust for Scotland who saved it from imminent demolition. A print from the year 1880 shows the building as a coffee house with no sign of the arcade in front of which a Victorian shopfront had been imposed.

The tenement was bought by the merchant Thomas Gledstanes who built a southern extension, which carried the building over the pavement on the twin arches, in 1617. He and his family then lived in one of the flats. Restoration by the Trust has enabled beam and board ceilings, brightly painted with flowers and fruit, to be brought back to life and has also revealed original painted wall decoration of the 17th century.

Gladstone's Land was leased to the Saltire Society as their headquarters and as a centre for the study of Scottish culture. By 1980 they had removed to other premises and the Trust took the opportunity to recreate a typical 17th century merchant's house on the first floor and to turn the ground floor into equally typical booths, or small shops, of the same period. The old building thus became the Trust's Old Town House in contrast to its New Town Georgian House in Charlotte Square (q.v.), both of which provide the means of looking back through history to an ancestral Edinburgh full of charm and interest to the modern visitor.

Holyrood Palace

In the early years of the 12th century the King, David I, was hunting in the extensive forest which stretched on every side around the Castle rock. Rescued from an attacking stag, according to tradition, by the appearance of a cross, or rood, between its antlers, he immediately vowed to found a religious house there in honour of 'the Holy Cross, the Virgin Mary and All Saints.' The ruins of the great Augustinian Abbey erected by the king can be seen today beside the palace.

It became the practice of the Scottish kings periodically to leave Edinburgh Castle (q.v.) on its high, defensive site and to lodge for a time in the guest house of the Abbey. It was, however, James IV (1488–1513) who decided to build a royal palace for himself and his successors and he made the guest house the nucleus of his new royal residence. To the completed Palace he brought his bride, Margaret Tudor, the daughter of Henry VII of England, in 1503. The original building is the north-west tower of the present Palace of Holyroodhouse, and it has become inseparably associated with the tragic reign

The Palace of Holyroodhouse is a royal residence and the most famous of Edinburgh's historic houses.

of Mary, Queen of Scots (1542–87). Early in her life it was sacked by the Earl of Hertford when her marriage treaty with the future Edward VI of England was annulled by the Scottish Parliament. Later, when she had married Henry, Lord Darnley, the Palace witnessed the murder of her Italian secretary, David Rizzio, in 1566. His body was left at the doorway of the Queen's Audience Chamber where an inscribed brass plate has been let into the floor. A year later Darnley too had been murdered and Mary was then married to the Earl of Bothwell in Holyrood Abbey.

Mary's son, James VI, brought his bride, Anne of Denmark, to the Palace for her coronation, and it was while he was in residence here that the news was brought to him that Queen Elizabeth was dead and that he was King of England. Leaving for London immediately, he did not return to his Scottish palace, and then only for a short visit, for fourteen years.

Charles I, James's son, was crowned in the Abbey in 1633, but Cromwell's soldiers were quartered in the Palace after Charles's execution and did considerable damage to the building.

Although Charles II had been crowned at Scone, he did not return to Scotland after the Restoration. A notable reconstruction and extension of Holyrood Palace was, however, carried out on the King's instructions, the architect being Sir William Bruce. The west front had been rebuilt by Cromwell but this was pulled down and re-erected to Bruce's new classical designs and linked to a south-west tower similar to that which had been built on the other side. Around the courtyard between the two towers the Palace as it now stands was

The north-west tower of Holyrood Palace which was built for James V in 1530 and which contains the historic apartments.

built, the cipher of Charles II, who never saw the work, being incorporated in the plaster ceilings and other parts of the fabric. His brother, the Duke of York and later James VII and II, stayed here when appointed High Commissioner.

Following the Union of the Parliaments in 1707 the Palace lost its importance as a royal dwelling and only reappears in history on such occasions as the single, glittering ball given in the Long Gallery by Prince Charles Edward in 1745 and then, from 1795 for several years when it was occupied, on two separate visits, by Charles X of France who came, seeking the sanctuary afforded by the Abbey, as a debtor after his financial ruin caused by his vain attempts to counter the French Revolution. (See Baberton House).

When George IV ended its neglect in 1822, he was the first monarch to cross its threshold since Charles II, and its full resuscitation took place when Queen Victoria made it once more a royal palace later in the 19th century. The State Apartments beside the Long Gallery (with its one hundred and eleven portraits of Scottish kings for painting which Charles II had paid £120 a year to the Dutch artist, de Wet) are particularly associated with the Queen and Prince Albert. They contain 17th century tapestries and a harpsichord of the same period. In the Throne Room are a painting of Charles I by Van Dyke and a late portrait of King George V.

The Palace of Holyroodhouse is regularly used, as her residence when in Edinburgh, by the present Queen, and annually in May by her representative, the Lord High Commissioner to the General Assembly of the Church of Scotland.

Huntly House

Huntly House, with its steeply pitched and deeply angled roof, its acutely pointed gables and its corbelled, timber upper floors, stands picturesquely on the south side of the Canongate next door to Acheson House (q.v.) and opposite the Canongate Tolbooth. A colloquial name for this house, which consisted originally of three houses which were linked together in 1570, was the Speaking House on account of several panels with Latin Mottoes on the facade. Those to be seen today are copies of the originals

The stone- and timber-fronted Huntly House which is now a municipal museum.

which are preserved within the building, the English translation of one being 'As you are master of your tongue, so am I master of my ears.'

This example of Old Town domestic architecture, which takes its name from a Dowager Countess of Huntly who once lived in a flat here, has been restored twice in the 20th century. Wood panelling from demolished houses in the Cowgate and painted ceiling beams from Pinkie House in Musselburgh have been used in the interior. Huntly House has for many years been a municipal museum and contains a wealth of artefacts relating to the city and its citizens in former times, including reconstructions of typical Old Town rooms of various periods and an impressive collection of large and brightly painted shop signs.

James Court

James, or James's, Court is to be found on the north side of the Lawnmarket. In the 1720s a speculative builder (or joiner as Robert Chambers calls him) called James Brownhill, who gave his own Christian name to it when completed, created an open court in which to build tenement flats on the northern side. To make room for this improved method of building around an open square he had first to sweep away some narrow, traditional closes, including that in which Lord Fountainhall, the 17th century judge, had lived. The Brownhill walls rose to at least six storeys from the courtyard but on the other side, where the ground slopes down in line with The Mound, the sheer cliff of masonry manages to incorporate another two. Inside well-designed stairs were approached through finely-moulded doorways.

Before the advent of gracious living in the as yet unbuilt New Town, this measure of spacious living was now becoming possible in the cramped and crowded Old Town for the fashionable few, and some famous names are associated with James Court. The inhabitants, says Chambers, 'were all persons of consequence in society' who, 'although each had but a single floor of four or five rooms and a kitchen, kept a clerk to record their names and proceedings, had a scavenger of their own . . . and had balls and parties among themselves exclusively.' David Hume, the great Scottish historian and philosopher, whom we shall meet again when the lure of the New Town had become too strong to be resisted, lived for a time in James Court. After him, in the same flat, came the most illustrious of its tenants, Boswell and Dr Johnson, the former entertaining there the latter when he had cajoled him into taking, in 1773, the highroad in the opposite direction to the one he considered so beneficial to every Scotsman. From here they set out on their tour to the Hebrides about which they were both to write memorable accounts after their safe return.

A later arrival on the scene was Patrick Geddes (see Ramsay Lodge) with his improvement plans, but not before the entire west

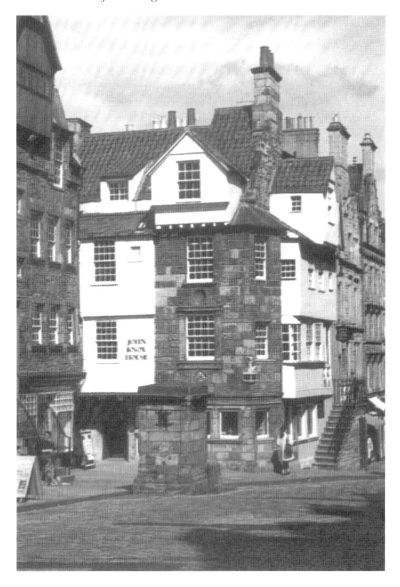

John Knox House, one of Edinburgh's finest and best-known historic buildings near the foot of the High Street. Moubray House, with the Fountain Well in front, is on the left.

side of the square, which included the apartments of Hume and Boswell, had been destroyed by fire in the mid-19th century and rebuilt in 1860 as offices of the Free Church of Scotland which are entered from The Mound. Patrick Geddes (whose decision to live in such, by then, insalubrious surroundings was at that time a courageous and unprecedented one) carried out his rehabilitation scheme for James Court as part of his restoration work in the Royal Mile.

John Knox House

John Knox, the intrepid Scottish Reformer and minister of the High Kirk of St. Giles, had his manse (pulled down when the City Chambers were extended) in Warriston Close. The fact, however, that he had become associated with the house which now bears his name was largely responsible for its preservation when faced with the threat of demolition, from which fate it was rescued by the Free Church of Scotland who purchased the building in the 19th century. Although it is unlikely that John Knox actually lived in it, there is a possibility that he may have died in it.

Built during the 15th century and one of the most picturesque buildings in the Royal Mile, it projects southwards across the pavement at the foot of the High Street and is surmounted by timber galleries and gables. Below a window are prominently displayed the initials of James Mossman, goldsmith to Mary Queen of Scots, and his wife Mariota Arres. John Geddie describes him as 'a zealous Catholic and Queen's man, who afterwards suffered on the scaffold ... for his attachment to the cause of Mary Stewart.' A small effigy on the corner to the right of the initials represents Moses standing on a sundial and pointing to the word 'God' in the three languages of Greek, Latin and English superimposed upon a golden-rayed sun.

Restoration of the interior has revealed painted panels and traces of early plaster finishing on the walls. It was traditional in medieval practice to cover inside walls with a thin coat of limewashed plaster which did not conceal the rough texture of the masonry beneath. In 1990 stone booths discovered on the south side at ground floor

The figure of Moses standing on a sundial on the walls of John Knox House. He is pointing to the word God in three languages on a gilded sun.

level are the only known late medieval shops to have survived in Scotland.

The house is now owned by the Church of Scotland and administered along with the Netherbow Centre next door.

Lady Stair's House

A lintel-stone bearing a scroll with the date 1622 and the words FEARE THE LORD AND DEPART FROM EVILL marks the entrance to Lady Stair's House. The initials beneath the scroll are those of its builder Sir William Gray of Pittendrum and his wife Gidia Smith, Gidia (or Egidia) being the daughter of Sir John Smith of Grothall, near Craigleith, who was provost of the city in 1643. Sir William Gray, a wealthy merchant, suffered for his support of the Marquis of Montrose during the Wars of the Covenant, resulting in his premature death in 1648.

One of the best-known buildings in Edinburgh, it stands in Lady Stair's Close (called Lady Gray's Close while the widow of Sir William Gray was resident there) on the north side of the Lawn-market. Closes were usually given the name of the most prominent person living in them and, when they left or died, the close would take the name of the occupant considered to be next in line of status and importance, a custom which explains the apparent existence of an unduly large number of closes in the Old Town. On the gable of Lady Stair's house a panel records its restoration in 1897 by George S. Aitken, FSA Scot., for Lord Rosebery who was a descendant of the Grays and had purchased the building for this purpose at the instigation of Patrick Geddes. He then, in 1907, presented the re-edified structure to the City. Their combined efforts resulted in something of an over-restoration of this plain and unadorned old property, iron balconies, elaborately pedi-mented windows and tall chimneys now being set somewhat chaoti-cally about the building. At the same time neighbouring closes were demolished to give the house some elbow-room and a more commanding appearance.

A principal feature of the interior is the large dining hall with an oak staircase leading up to a musicians' gallery. A stone stair with steps of uneven height, known as a trip stair, has been preserved as an example of an early form of burglar alarm. An intruder, unfamiliar with the building, would be liable to stumble and so reveal his presence. Stairs of this kind can also be found in some old English houses. In Penfound Manor in Cornwall, home of the family of that name for five hundred years, mentioned in the Domesday Book and the oldest inhabited house in England, the main staircase, constructed of wood in 1589, was similarly designed and also had some steps sloping in different directions as an added obstacle.

In Lady Stair's time the house had a terraced garden descend-ing towards the Nor' Loch and a 19th century print shows the mansion well hemmed within its ancient close with no hint of the embellishments, now a hundred years old, with which it was later to be weighed down. The first Lady Stair to be associated with the house was Elizabeth, the Dowager Countess, who held court here in the earlier part of the 18th century, and in 1789 it was offered for sale in the *Edinburgh Advertiser*, the upset price being £250.

Now the Writers' Museum, Lady Stair's House contains portraits, prints, letters and other relics of Burns, Scott and Stevenson, including Sir Walter Scott's dining table in a reconstruction of an early 19th century room.

Milne's Court in the Lawnmarket - the first attempt to provide more space in the overcrowded Old Town and now restored as University Residences.

Milne's Court

The first attempt to overcome the congested life of the narrow closes was the creation, in the closing years of the 17th century, of Milne's Court. The closes had evolved as garden ground was pressed into use for additional tenement building to meet the housing needs of an increasing Old Town population. The Court was the work of Robert Mylne, a member of that famous family of master masons to the kings of Scotland, and he had no hesitation in casting down old Lawnmarket closes to obtain the necessary space. Only part of his building work has survived but it rises to a height of eight storeys on the north side above The Mound from which its crowsteps and gables can be seen. Within the open court-yard an exterior stair leads up to a third-floor moulded entrance doorway to the north, while on the east side is a projecting turnpike stairtower. The six-storey south, or Lawnmarket, front is extant also with the date 1690 above the entrance to the pend.

In 1968 Milne's Court was restored as Halls of Residence for the University of Edinburgh.

Moray House

It could well be said that this most interesting 'noble mansion', as it has been called, on the south side of the Canongate, stands at the heart of Old Edinburgh history. Erected in 1628 by Mary, Dowager Countess of Home, it was given by her to her daughter, the Countess of Moray, in 1645. The house remained in the possession of that family for two hundred years, but in 1648 it was already embarking on its historic destiny with Oliver Cromwell lodged within its walls. Cromwell was back in two years' time, after his victory at the Battle of Dunbar, holding levees and issuing orders, in John Geddie's words, 'to the perverted, unruly Scots.'

It was in the same year, 1650, that the Marquis of Montrose was carried, bound and on a cart, up the Canongate to his death at the Cross of Edinburgh after his capture by the Covenanters. The story is well known of how, as he passed Moray House, a wedding party was assembled on the balcony which can still be seen corbelled out ornamentally at first-floor level on the gable facing the street. There stood the Marquis of Argyle with his son, Lord Lorne, who had just been married to Lady Mary Stuart, a daughter of the Earl of Moray, and their guests, but the statement that they were exulting over the humiliation of Montrose and spitting down upon him as he approached his fate with a serenity that was not unnoticed by the staring crowds, is almost certainly a fabrication. A year and a decade later it was Argyle, who directed the affairs of Scotland during the Commonwealth, who was borne in his turn to his execution at the same Mercat Cross.

In the early years of the 18th century, when rumours were rife of Scotland's betrayal and the removal of her parliament, Moray House was the residence of Lord Chancellor Seafield. This Scottish earl was an active player in the Union drama and it was he who made the often quoted remark 'that it was the end of an auld sang' when, in 1707, the Union of the Parliaments became an accomplished fact. Standing forlornly behind Holyrood Road is the 17th century summer house in which part of the clandestine Union manoeuvring took place. The signing of the Act is said to have been carried out partly in the summer house and partly in a High Street cellar while the cries, says Grant, 'of the exasperated mob rang in the streets.' The pantile-roofed, stone-built summer house and a 'sparkling fountain' were originally the principal features of the Moray House gardens which were rich in fruit trees and arbours, one of them being called Queen Mary's Bower. The pavilion itself had a lean-to conservatory on the west side and the entrance on the north. Two stone greyhounds – the supporters in the Moray Arms – surmounted the building and are now detached and kept inside where a large plaque records the history of the summer house which is now entered through the former site of the conservatory.

Giant pyramidal finials tower above the two stout gate-piers which stand at the entrance to Moray House in the Canongate just east of the balconied gable at the side of which a semi-octagonal turnpike stair-tower projects into the forecourt approach area. Much of the fine interior has vanished but the domed Renaissance ceiling with intricately carved plasterwork and pendants still remains in the room behind the balcony as well as painted panelling in the Cromwell Room.

In 1847 the house was taken over by the United Free Church of Scotland and used as a school and teachers' training college. Thereafter it was incorporated in the Moray House College of Education for which large additional buildings, approached from Holyrood Road and occupying much of the original garden ground, were constructed just before the First World War.

Moubray House

Immediately to the west of John Knox House (q.v.) adjoins the dark, heavy stonework of Moubray House rising, its windows spaced irregularly in the walls, through four floors to an oversailing wooden attic storey at the top. It is entered by steep forestairs and a much later moulded doorway. The house, called after the original builder, Andrew Moubray, dates back to the 15th century and predates the building of John Knox House next door with which it shares its eastern wall, but has been altered and enlarged, especially on the street frontage, since then.

It was here that the first prominent Scottish portrait painter, George Jamesone, sometimes called the 'Scottish Van Dyck', had his studio on an upper floor, and a plaque carved by Belle M. Kilgour in 1964, rather high on the wall, displays a head of the artist and his dates of birth and death (1590–1644). The son of an Aberdeen mason, he was born in that city in a now demolished house which his father had built in the Schoolhill.

The painting usually considered to be Jamesone's masterpiece is his portrait of Lady Mary Erskine, sixth Countess Marischal, at the age of twenty-nine, which hangs in the National Gallery of Scotland. He is thought to have attended Marischal College in Aberdeen and subsequently to have travelled to Antwerp where he was either apprenticed to Rubens or simply copied a number of his works. He is also known to have visited Italy. He was created King's Limner in Scotland and a portrait by him of Charles I is at Drummond Castle. Being on the king's side, he was imprisoned for refusing to sign the National Covenant and on his death was buried in an unmarked grave in Greyfriars Churchyard.

Moubray House, which contains painted walls and ceilings and a fine plaster ceiling on the first floor, was acquired and restored by the Cockburn Association in 1911.

Panmure House

Panmure House is reached from Little Lochend Close in the Canongate where, its only ornament its crowstepped gables, it has stood since the second half of the 17th century. Access to this

Hidden within Little Lochend Close in the Canongate is Panmure House, formerly the townhouse of the earls of Panmure and later the home of Adam Smith.

large, L-plan building is through a wide, flattened arch in its retaining wall, the archway being closed with a double-leaved gate resembling an old Scottish yett though the bars do not, as in a yett, interlace. Steps ascend to a small open forecourt and the entrance doorway of the house.

This was the townhouse of the Earls of Panmure, James, the fourth earl, being a fervid Jacobite and strongly opposed to the Union of the Parliaments in 1707. Deprived of his estates in Angus as a consequence, he went into exile and died in Paris. The attainted James was succeeded by his nephew, William Maule, about 1743 when he took up residence in the house which after his death passed to the Countess of Aberdeen.

For the last twelve years of his life Panmure House was the home of Adam Smith (1723–90), author of *An Enquiry into the Nature and Causes of the Wealth of Nations*. The great Scottish economist, for whom the Duke of Buccleuch had been instrumental in obtaining an appointment as Commissioner of Customs, was, says Chambers, 'abstracted and scholarly' and 'ill fitted for common worldly life.' Apparently this was true to such an extent that it was once said of him, 'How strange to think of one who has written so well on the principles of exchange and barter – he is obliged to get a friend to buy his horse-corn for him!' He died in the house and was buried in the Canongate Churchyard.

There are two bronze plaques beside the door. The larger gives the information:

> The former town house of the Earls of Panmure and also of Adam Smith LL.D., author of 'The Wealth of Nations' who lived here 1778–1790. Was renovated in 1957 and presented by Roy Herbert Thomson, Esq., Chairman of The Scotsman Publications Ltd., to The Rev. Ronald Selby Wright, D.D., for the Canongate Boys' Club and was opened by H.R.H. The Princess Royal accompanied by His Grace the Duke of Hamilton, K.T., President, and dedicated by The Rt. Rev. The Moderator, Sir George F. Macleod, Bart., D.D., on 6th October 1957.
>
> J. Wilson Paterson, Esq., Architect.

Above is a small tablet stating that the building was visited by the Duke of Edinburgh on 1st July 1958.

Panmure House, which was a laundry at the beginning of the present century, is now used by the Social Work Department as a non-residential youth centre.

Queensberry House

A long, strange and tragic story belongs to Queensberry House, standing, a high and starkly uninviting pile, opposite White-foord House (q.v.) in the Canongate. It was built in 1681 by Lord Hatton, one of the Maitlands of Lauderdale (see Brunstane House) who sold it to William, first Duke of Queensberry shortly after its completion. James, the second duke, transferred his allegiance from the old house of Stuart to William of Orange and was later one of the Commissioners appointed to carry out the unpopular Treaty of Union for which he received the sum of just over £12,000. As a consequence Queensberry House became the target of mob violence and the duke left Edinburgh hurriedly, to return, however, when passions had cooled, as one of the representative peers of Scotland with his own house in Kensington when he attended Parliament in London.

It was the misfortune of the Dukes of Queensberry that congenital insanity made it likely from time to time that an heir would be unable to inherit the dukedom from his father, and this was the case with the eldest son of the second duke. He was, says Grant, 'an idiot of the most wretched kind' and was confined in an apartment in the west wing of the house with the windows boarded up to prevent his being seen. On the day on which the union with the English Parliament was made absolute the people took to the streets and made for the Parliament House where the duke and his entire household were assembled. 'Hearing all unusually still in the vast house', as the attendant of the deranged son had gone as well, the madman escaped from his prison and started roaming from room to room, coming at last to the kitchen where an unsuspecting houseboy, 'a little turnspit', sat quietly by the fire. When the family and their retainers returned home they found the meat taken from the fire and, in its place, the half-roasted servant boy whom the crazed son was attempting to devour. Every effort was made, though without success, to prevent the terrible incident from becoming known, and it was soon being widely regarded as 'a judgment upon him for his odious share in the Union.'

About 1730 (a pleasanter story) the Duchess of Queensberry, the wife of the third duke, gave shelter in the house to the English poet, John Gay, for whom it proved conveniently situated, being near the circulating library kept by Allan Ramsay (see Ramsay Lodge), the Scottish poet, in the Luckenbooths beside St. Giles, and even closer to the changehouse, or tavern, kept by Jenny Ha' on the other side of the street.

On the death of the third duke, the inherited madness having reappeared in his eldest son who had committed suicide, the title passed to his cousin, the Earl of March, a dissolute character known to history as 'Old Q'. The contents of Queensberry House, of considerable value, were largely removed to Gosford House, the residence of the Earl of Wemyss and March at the present day, and the old mansion, stripped of its many interesting and decorative features, was

The much-altered Queensberry House – a grim old building with a long history at the foot of the Canongate. The front of the house faces south to Holyrood Road.

sold to the Government in 1801 when, after the unfortunate addition of a further storey and the loss of its ornamental chimneys and roof, it was converted into barracks. This did not happen, however, before the house had one last private occupant. This was Sir James William Montgomery, Lord Chief Baron of the Scottish Exchequer, an office from which he resigned two years before his death in 1803. He was also Solicitor General and, afterwards, Lord Advocate.

Sir James lived, says Cockburn in his *Memorials*, 'in Queensberry House in the Canongate and I believe was the last gentleman who resided in that historical mansion, which, though now one of the asylums of destitution, was once the brilliant abode of rank and fashion and political intrigue.' Cockburn wished that the street 'could be refreshed again by the habitual sight of the Lord Chief Baron's family and company, and the gorgeous carriage, and the tall and well-dressed figure, in the old style, of his Lordship himself.'

About the middle of the 19th century this house which had witnessed events that had changed the course of Scottish history became, as Cockburn had lamented, a House of Refuge for the Destitute and subsequently a geriatric hospital. The Hospital closed in 1995 when the building (which faces south with its back to the Canongate) was bought by Scottish & Newcastle Breweries. In 1998 it was included in the large site acquired from them to become the location of the Scottish Parliament, the intention being to demolish the brewery buildings, erect a new Parliament House and use Queensberry House to provide additional accommodation.

Ramsay Lodge

The complex of buildings known as Ramsay Lodge was the brainchild of Patrick Geddes (1854–1932), who did so much to rescue many of the Old Town buildings and to bring new life back into the Royal Mile which had degenerated into a slum after the creation of the New Town, for which he is only now beginning to receive recognition. In the centre, and best seen from the north or Princes Street Gardens side, is the octagonal house which was built by Allan Ramsay (see Queensberry House) whose statue is on the other side of the valley beside the floral clock. The little house is engulfed within the later and larger buildings.

Ramsay Lodge, the 'Goose-pie' of the poet Allan Ramsay, in the centre of late 19th-century buildings by Patrick Geddes beside the Castle Esplanade.

Allan Ramsay, poet and author of *The Gentle Shepherd*, was a familiar figure on the streets of 18th century Edinburgh and chose a site at the entrance to the Castle Esplanade on which to build his house away from the noise and clatter of the High Street and with a splendid open outlook to the Firth of Forth. Because of its shape the fine new residence was soon being called the 'Goose-pie', a name which the poet keenly resented. Taking the opportunity of a visit one day from Lord Elibank to express his indignation, he received little consolation from the reply, 'Indeed, Allan, when you are in it, I think it is not far wrong!' In 1741 he made a gift of the house to his son, also called Allan Ramsay and one of the foremost artists of his time both in Scotland and in England where he became portrait painter to George III. Allan Ramsay, senior, who was born in 1686, died in the house in 1758 and was buried in Greyfriars Churchyard.

In addition to a picturesque group of flats, in one of which he himself and his wife lived, Patrick Geddes created a Hall of Residence here for the University in which the Common Room has a series of twelve mural paintings by John Duncan (1866–1945) which are being retained within the modern flats into which the Hall is being converted.

Regent Morton's House

In Blackfriars Street, in the heart of the Old Town, stands the house of the Earls of Morton, built towards the end of the 16th century. It has escaped the surrounding demolition work and still displays its ogival-headed doorway, above which is a weathered shield surmounted by a coronet and flanked by unicorns, in the projecting stair-tower. Savages were the traditional supporters in the Morton coat-of-arms, but the building is anciently documented as having belonged to the Morton family. It had an oversailing timber gallery above the street frontage but this disappeared in the late 19th century.

John Geddie says that the house is 'traditionally assigned to the Regent Morton', the fourth earl who for five years acted as regent during the minority of James VI but who finally lost life and lands for allegedly conspiring to bring about the death of Darnley. It has now been restored as the High Street Youth Hostel.

Sempill House

Sempill, or Semple, House stands in Sempill's Close in Castlehill, on the eastern side of the Outlook Tower, and bears the date 1638. A short flight of stone steps leads down to two doors, that on the left giving access to a turnpike stair-tower, and there are carved lintels above both doors. In 1743 the building was bought by Hugh, Lord Sempill, but it came into the possession of the Clerks of Penicuik in

1755. The mansion behind the stair tower was demolished in 1965 to make way for the building of a kitchen extension for New College.

St. John's House

The only surviving house in the short St. John's Street, off the Canongate, and built in the mid-18th century, St. John's House (No. 21), with its Maltese Crosses on the door and gate and its small front garden, is now the Headquarters of the Priory of Scotland of The Order of St. John.

No. 1 Surgeons Square

In Surgeons Square, to the north of Drummond Street and formerly entered from High School Yards from which there is now no access although a pend leads through on the south side of the former High School, the old Surgeon's Hall, altered and heightened by an additional storey, can still be seen. A garden lay in front of the Hall and at either side of it two houses were built in the 1770s. One of these houses, that on the eastern side, has survived though it is considerably altered and an extra storey has been added. This house is known as No. 1 Surgeons Square and may have been designed by William Mylne.

Tweeddale House

For over a hundred years the Marquises of Tweeddale had their townhouse on the south side of the High Street with a garden and an avenue of lime trees which extended to the Cowgate. Built in the second half of the 16th century, it was bought about a hundred years later by Sir William Bruce, Scotland's first great classical architect, who made considerable alterations before selling it in his turn to the Hays, Earls and later Marquises of Tweeddale of Yester House in East Lothian.

Tweeddale House in the High Street. The classically-columned doorway was an 18th century addition.

Robert Adam was employed in the mid-18th century to 'modernise' the house in line with the prevailing style, and in the closing years of that century it was acquired from the Tweeddale family by the British Linen Bank. On the bank's removal to St. Andrew Square in the New Town it was purchased by the publishers Oliver & Boyd by one of whose successors it has been restored.

It was in the close leading to Tweeddale House that, during the period of the bank's occupancy, an unsolved murder which aroused keen interest at the time took place in 1806. On the evening of 13th November the expiring William Begbie, a porter in the bank's employment, was found there with a knife through his heart by a little girl who had been sent out, says Grant, 'by her mother with a kettle to get water for tea from the Fountain Well.' This was violence with robbery indeed, and about £4000 in notes, which he was bringing from the Leith branch of the bank, was taken, and not a sound had been heard by anyone. Although five hundred guineas was offered as a reward and every effort made to track down the criminal, he was never found. Several months afterwards, however, three men discovered a weatherbeaten roll of bank notes in a wall where Drummond Place was subsequently built on the estate of Bellevue. The notes were identified as part of the Begbie robbery and the men were given £200 each for their honesty by the bank. Suspicion fell eventually on a known thief, but he died before his guilt could be established.

Tweeddale House stands at the foot of Tweeddale Close and is entered through a porch, flanked by Roman Doric columns, which was an addition of about 1799. In the close is a small, low building which is said to be the last sedan chair 'garage' left in Edinburgh.

Whitefoord House

Whitefoord House was not the first building on its site near the foot of the Canongate. It replaced a mansion, belonging to the Seton family, which has come down in history as Lord Seton's Ludging, and it was in that house that Henry, Lord Darnley, stayed when he came to Edinburgh in 1565 for his marriage to Mary, Queen of Scots.

The present building, Whitefoord House, was the work of Robert Mylne and was constructed in 1769 for Sir John Whitefoord, Bart., of Ballochmyle in Ayrshire, one of the patrons of Robert Burns, who died in the house in 1803.

Its most famous occupant was Sir William Macleod Bannatyne, the Scottish judge. He lived to the age of ninety and could recall his father's involvement in 'the '45'. Sir William was one of the last surviving members of the Mirror Club, one of numerous such institutions in 18th century Edinburgh which were proverbial for the nightly conviviality to which members of the legal profession were particularly addicted. He died in the house in 1833 and the building was afterwards used as a type foundry.

In 1910 this historic mansion, retaining the name of Whitefoord House, became, together with CALLANDER HOUSE on its immediate west which was built by Sir John Callander of Craigforth at much the same time, a home for war veterans, many of whom at that time were living in the Grassmarket in huts as they had no other accommodation. Today it is occupied by about 120 men, and of that number some would otherwise be homeless. In 1977 an appeal was launched for funds to enable extensive repairs and improvements to be carried out for the benefit of the residents.

The mansionhouse, together with Callander House to which it is joined, is set back from the Canongate within a courtyard and has three storeys, a basement and a projecting pedimented portico.

At No. 36 Calton Road at the back of the Canongate the former Balmoral Brewery was converted into sixteen flats in 1983.

Part II
The New Town

The 14th century French chronicler, Jean Froissart, impressed by what he saw on a visit to Edinburgh, called the old, grey, straggling town 'the Paris of Scotland'. Understandably, this name did not gain wide acceptance, but by the end of the 18th century another capital city was being invoked to describe the splendid, classical New Town that was then in course of building, and to provide a name which, even if only slightly less fanciful than the first, would this time be used and remembered right down to the present day and which had particular reference to the Calton Hill with its monuments and columns – the Athens of the North.

After decades of doubt, debate and indecision it was at last agreed that the old Royalty should be extended and a well-designed, fashionable residential addition laid out across the fields and open country on the further side of the Nor', or North, Loch valley.

The moving spirit behind the eventual implementation of this plan was George Drummond, six times Lord Provost of the city, who, having been born in 1687 and dying in 1766 at the age of 79, lived just long enough to witness the commencement of the historic but expensive undertaking. In 1766 the Town Council launched a competition for a new town plan and out of the six which were submitted chose that of the young Scottish architect James Craig (1744–95), a nephew of the poet James Thomson, whose reward was a gold medal and the freedom of the city in a silver box. The following year Craig laid the foundation stone of the first house (in Rose Court, now Thistle Court) lying to the rear of George Street on the northern side, a 'bribe' of £20 having been accepted by the new proprietor for the privilege of being the front runner to the exposed and windswept site. Access had been obtained by the building of the North Bridge, and a 'mud brig', afterwards called The Mound, came later, created from the 'travelled earth' dug out for the foundations of the Princes Street houses.

The plan was a simple one – a principal street, George Street, terminating in squares at either end and flanked, in Princes Street

Original long, narrow gardens at the back of Great King Street, with the back of Northumberland Street behind, in the Second New Town.

and Queen Street, by terraces on lower ground to the south and north. Exemption from rates was the inducement to build the initial house in Princes Street! This was the late Adam period and the influence of Robert (1728–92), who introduced an elegant Greek classicism to interior as well as exterior design, is not as strong as it might have been had he lived longer. Most of his work was finished by other hands (and altered due to insufficiency of funds).

Princes Street, so well known today as the principal thoroughfare in the city, was originally a long row of rather plain and wholly residential terraced houses. Well before the middle of the 19th century, however, shopkeeping and other public or commercial uses were forcing the inhabitants to leave them and move on, mainly in a northerly direction, just as (although there are also profound dissimilarities in the comparison) an earlier generation had ventured out in the same direction to create the First New Town on virgin ground. A few upper elevations of original buildings can still be detected in Princes Street above the multifarious shopfronts, but evidence, commemorative or surviving, of their first proprietors is not to be found in what has been called 'the most magnificent esplanade in Europe.'

At the turn of the century the Second New Town, further down the northward-facing slope, was being considered, the prime mover being another Lord Provost, David Stewart, a merchant and banker in the city. He himself feuded land to the north of Queen Street and put forward his ideas to the Heriot Trust who owned practically all of it, in the year of Robert Adam's death. A layout somewhat similar to that of the First New Town was planned (the principal architects being Robert Reid (1774–1856), the last King's Architect in Scotland, and the Town Council's Superintendent of Works William Sibbald (d. 1809)) and took shape in the early years of the 19th century. This time the main axis was Great King Street with Drummond Place and Royal Circus, with their gardens, as terminal features and with lesser streets to north and south.

As the century advanced, ground to the west as far as the Moray estates and eastward to the Calton Hill was developed until the whole New Town of Edinburgh became, if rather later in date, considerably larger than Bath, Cheltenham, York and other English cities of Georgian architectural renown.

The building of Edinburgh's New Town was by any standards a remarkable achievement, and it still retains much of its residential character at the end of the 20th century in spite of some deliberate civic vandalism. But damage to the environmental totality created by its originators can be deceptive and concealed. Apart from the blatant (though sometimes necessary) practice of retaining existing street frontages while destroying what lies behind them (i.e. the houses themselves), the rear gardens, not visible to the passer-by, can be abused, particularly by the cutting down of large, mature and still viable trees. All such New Town garden trees are covered by an official preservation order, but permission to remove them can on many occasions be too easily obtained without any statutory obligation to replace them with other suitable varieties. The trees having been disposed of, incompatible building can then be intruded in the denuded garden. This was a situation which occurred more fre-

The destruction of three Great King Street back gardens in 1967 and the intrusion of incompatible modern buildings (cf. previous illustration).

quently in the 1960s and early '70s before enlightened conservation had come to be seen as sensible and asset-saving, rather than backward-looking, civic policy. The New Town was succeeded by serried rows of soundly-built stone tenements, echoing all the previous Scottish architectural styles, in the long, Imperial, Victorian era.

The New Town had its detractors, however, among them Lord Cockburn, and Sir Daniel Wilson who, in his *Memorials of Edinburgh in the Olden Time*, called the plan commonplace and not carefully aligned with the contours of the ground. But it was praised by the English Ruskin in his Edinburgh lectures and, in more recent times, by the Scottish writer George Scott-Moncrieff who said: 'The end of the eighteenth century and the beginning of the nineteenth saw the birth and growth of the New Town of Edinburgh. It is the outstanding phase of the City's history since the Reformation. In the classical parlance of the day it was her Augustan Age, and she the Modern Athens.'

Abercromby Place

In this shallow crescent in the Second New Town, the first curved street to be built in Edinburgh, the houses face south to the eastern section of Queen Street Gardens. Its shape aroused so much public

Ornamental ironwork outside a house in Abercromby Place. The balcony was intended for flowers and plants.

interest that Cockburn noted in his *Memorials* that many people came to stand and stare at it. Building began in the opening years of the 19th century – a main central block terminating in higher end pavilions with Nelson Street as an intersection halfway along.

At No. 21 William Edmondstoun Aytoun (1813–65) was born. Professor of Rhetoric at the University of Edinburgh and a famous contributor to *Blackwood's Magazine*, he had married Jane, the daughter of Professor John Wilson (Christopher North) (see Christopher North's House), one of whose students he had been in earlier years. In 1853, after leaving their first home at No. 1 Inverleith Terrace which was then occupied by the young Robert Louis Stevenson and his parents (see Howard Place and Heriot Row), the Aytouns moved to No. 16 Great Stuart Street, a house which he described as being 'big enough to lodge a patriarch.' Aytoun was known as 'one of the standing wits of the Law Courts' prior to exchanging the legal profession for the academic one in which he spent the rest of his active life. Both he and his father-in-law were buried in the Dean Cemetery.

William Henry Playfair, one of the later New Town architects, lived for a time at No. 17 Abercromby Place.

Albany Street

In what was known originally as Albany Row, No. 2 and later No. 10 were occupied by Professor John Playfair (1748–1819), whose more famous nephew was the New Town architect William Henry Playfair who laid out the eastern development beyond the Calton Hill. In 1805 the elder Playfair was appointed to the chair of Natural Philosophy at Edinburgh University and thereafter lived principally in Burntisland in Fife but retained his townhouse in Albany Street as well.

W.H. Playfair designed the Professor's memorial monument on the Calton Hill outside the New Observatory, also designed by him, John Playfair having been President of the Astronomical Institution which was founded in 1812.

Atholl Crescent

One of the later New Town crescents and forming, with Coates Crescent, a gently curving oval cut by the central line of the main road to the west, Atholl Crescent lies on the south-eastern side of the two components. Ionic pilasters and balconies ornament the facade. It was built, on Heriot Trust ground, in 1824 by Thomas Bonnar, a New Town architect about whom very little is known. Even the date of his death, thought to be 1832, is uncertain.

The publisher of the later works of Sir Walter Scott, Robert Cadell (1788–1849), lived at No. 16. He was in partnership with Archibald Constable (see Trinity Grove and Craigcrook Castle) but after Constable's business failure he co-operated with Scott in the reissue of many of the novels, the copyright of which they had jointly purchased.

Lockhart, in his *Life of Scott*, describes how, in January 1830, Sir Walter went to Edinburgh 'for the purpose of executing his last will'. He stayed, for the first time in his native city, in a hotel, but found that 'the noise of the street disturbed him during the night.' The next day 'he was persuaded to remove to his bookseller's house in Atholl Crescent. In the apartment allotted to him there, he found several little pieces of furniture which some kind person had purchased for him at the sale in Castle Street, and which he presented to Mrs Cadell.' Writing to his daughter Sophia, Mrs Lockhart, he told her, 'I saw various things that belonged to poor No. 39. I had many sad thoughts on seeing and handling them – but they are in kind keeping, and I was glad they had not gone to strangers.' The next day there came on, says Lockhart, a storm of such severity that he had to remain under this friendly roof until the 9th of February and, his health by now beginning to give cause for some concern, 'his host perceived that he was unfit for any company but the quietest.' The will was signed on the 4th of February and deposited for safety in Mr Cadell's hands.

Robert Cadell also owned Ratho House in Midlothian, and it was here that his death occurred at the age of sixty-one.

Baxter's Place

During restoration work in 1977/8 large projecting shopfronts and a cinema were removed from the short terrace on the south side at the top of Leith Walk called, after its architect, Baxter's Place. The frontages of the few buildings here, on the south-eastern edge of the New Town, were then rebuilt to resemble as nearly as possible their original appearance of a little row of Georgian houses of three storeys with basements and attics. Large Doric pilasters run between the windows on the first and second floors of the two end blocks in this attractive development by John Baxter, Jnr., shortly before his death in 1798. A paved court has been laid out behind iron railings over the area which had been covered by the shop extensions.

Nos. 1–3 are known as Robert Stevenson House, No. 1 being the home of the lighthouse engineer Robert Stevenson, the grandfather of R.L.S., who died here, aged 78, in 1850, the year of Robert Louis' birth.

Calton Gaol Governor's House

Sometimes mistaken for Edinburgh Castle, the tall, turreted Gaol on the Calton Hill has disappeared, but the Governor's house was spared when Scotland's administrative centre, St. Andrew's House, replaced the prison in 1937. The original gaol, by Robert Adam, was completed in 1796 but was superseded on the same site by a new prison block in 1817 to the designs of Archibald Elliot, and it was that architect who, at the same time, built the Governor's House. Grant records that prisoners' workshops could be 'surveyed from a dark apartment in the house of the Governor without the observer being visible.'

No present-day use for this interesting building has yet been found.

Charlotte Square

The last part of the First New Town to be built was Charlotte Square, the plans being drawn up by Robert Adam in the ultimate year of his life. So it came about that what has been called one of the finest squares in Europe was largely the work of his successor, Robert Reid (1774–1856). The north side, however, is considered to be Adam's most outstanding architectural design, not only in Edinburgh but in Scotland, and was carried out almost exactly as he had himself envisaged it. Here is the 'palace front' concept at its best – the whole street being treated as a single unit. Grouped columns, paterae and other ornament beneath a pedi-

Part of Robert Adam's elegant facade at No. 6 Charlotte Square.

ment in the centre, giant wide pilasters above Venetian windows with balusters at first-floor level, and delicate Adam decoration including sphinxes at the roofline make the north facade stand out in excellence from the rest of the square. Here, as in several other New Town streets, can be seen iron link, or torch, extinguishers incorporated in the railing design beside the entrance steps to some of the houses, but these were possibly never used as gas street lighting was then being introduced in Edinburgh.

Robert Adam, born in Kirkcaldy and son of the builder and architect William Adam, became the leading exponent of late 18th century Georgian architecture in Britain, designing furniture and other interior embellishments for his country houses in Scotland and England. In addition to the north side of Charlotte Square, his Register House at the east end of Princes Street, completed (at the rear) after his death by Robert Reid, and the University (modified and completed by Playfair) remain as major examples of his work in the northern capital.

Not surprisingly, this upmarket enclave had residents of fame and prominence from the beginning. Lord Chief Commissioner William Adam, a nephew of Robert and his brothers and a friend of Scott, lived here, as did Sir William Fettes, founder of the school to which he gave his name, Lord Lister of medical pre-eminence, and the great Whig Solicitor General and memorialist, Henry Cockburn and, at a later date, Earl Haig (1861–1928), who commanded the British Army during the First World War, was born at No. 24. A member of the noted family of distillers who commenced their operations in Edinburgh beside the Water of Leith in the 18th century and became internationally famous for the production of whisky, Douglas Haig died in London but was buried in the ruins of Dryburgh Abbey near the Haigs' Border home of Bemersyde (see Glenogle House, Heriot Hill House and Broomfield).

Nos. 5, 6 and 7 Charlotte Square, in partial payment of estate duty, became the property of the National Trust for Scotland in 1966 following the death of the fifth Marquis of Bute, No. 5, which they had occupied as tenants since 1949, then becoming the Trust's headquarters and offices which are shortly to be moved to the south side of the square where six buildings (Nos 26-31) have now been purchased by the Trust. From them the Bute House Trust leased No. 6 which was given the name of BUTE HOUSE and, after appropriate alteration, established as the official residence of the Secretary of State for Scotland.

With financial assistance from the Baird Trust, the upper floors of No. 7 were taken over as the official residence of the Moderator of the General Assembly of the Church of Scotland and the remainder of the building was restored and furnished by The National Trust for Scotland as their New Town House. Now known as THE GEORGIAN HOUSE, it reveals, in the beautiful contents of its drawing- and dining-rooms and its well-equipped kitchen of the period, the family lifestyle of those who lived there in the late 18th century. Later they went on to carry out a similar plan in the Old Town at Gladstone's Land (q.v.)

The north side of Charlotte Square is seen at its best when viewed across an angle of the Garden, especially in Spring when it is carpeted with crocuses, which occupies the centre of the square.

Chester Street

B uilt in the 1860s, Chester Street is part of the Victorian development, still following the basic Georgian stylistic manner, which created Edinburgh's residential West End.

Here, in No. 25, lived William Chambers (1800–83) when Lord Provost of the city from 1867 to 1870. He and his brother, Robert, were born in Peebles of a family of woollen and cotton manufacturers. Their father enlarged the business, sometimes having, according to Grant, as many as 'a hundred looms at work'. Able therefore to give his sons a good local education, when he was later overtaken by financial difficulties and it was decided to move to Edinburgh the two brothers were able to set themselves up gradually but successfully as printers and booksellers. *Chambers' Journal*, which went out of publication only in the recent past, was started by William in 1832 and proved an immediate success, and it was his pioneering work in the field of cheap literature that brought fame as well as prosperity to the name of Chambers.

A scheme to restore the interior of the High Kirk of St. Giles by the removal of the partition walls by which it had been divided into three separate areas of worship was strongly supported by William Chambers. His last great act of benefaction to Edinburgh was the donation of £30,000 to meet the cost of that undertaking. Three days before St. Giles was re-opened, with the reconstructed interior which can still be seen today, William (his brother having predeceased him in 1870) died, after a long, industrious and productive life, in 1883.

Chambers Street, laid out in the early 1870s under the city improvement scheme with which William was closely identified, was, says Grant, 'worthily named after the Lord Provost.'

Drummond Place

Although called Drummond Square on John Ainslie's map of 1804, the first thing to be said is that, although it might at first sight be thought so, Drummond Place is not in fact square. Situated at the east end of Great King Street (q.v.), it has a curved east side and the rows to the north and south are longer than those on the east and west. The layout on the east side of the Second New Town was by Robert Reid, but Thomas Bonnar, Thomas Brown and other architects were also involved as the 19th century advanced to the end of its second decade. The style is similar to that of Great King Street, with the strategic placing of giant Ionic pilasters and thermal, or semicircular, attic windows on palace-front facades surrounding a central Garden which is of more than usual interest. The Excise Office, formerly the house of Bellevue which had been built on the same site to replace Drummond Lodge, the old vernacular mansion-house of Sir George Drummond (see Dundas House and Colinton Castle), ended its days enclosed by the railings of Drummond Place Garden and was demolished in 1845 when the Scotland Street railway tunnel was driven beneath it. Sir George's name seemed an apt one for these still remarkably quiet and elegant streets, and the word 'Place' may possibly have been borrowed from the French *Place*.

The most colourful resident of Drummond Place was undoubtedly the eccentric antiquary Charles Kirkpatrick Sharpe (c. 1781–1851). Born in Dumfriesshire, and having previously lived in Princes Street, he removed to No. 28 Drummond Place in 1835. Thirty years later, in the words of Robert Chambers, he had himself 'become, as it were, a tradition of Edinburgh.' His dress and manner belonged to the high fashion of his Regency youth and gave him a quaint and outmoded, if aristocratic, appearance. Quaint also and biting, says Chambers, was his wit though he was essentially 'good-natured and fond of merriment'. Characteristically of both, 'in jest upon his own peculiarity of voice' he designed a calling card for himself on which was printed nothing more than C sharp in musical notation.

C.K.S., as he was called, was a great collector of old curiosities and Jacobite relics, and No. 28, wrote James Grant, 'was one of the sights of Edinburgh to the select few who found admittance there.' At his death in 1851 the collection was dispersed and the auctioneers' catalogue ran to 'upwards of fifty pages'. He himself, aged 71, was 'laid amid his forefathers in the family burial-place in Annandale.'

Adam Black, publisher, Member of Parliament for the City, and Lord Provost of Edinburgh from 1843–48, lived at No. 38. In 1827 he bought the publishing rights of the *Encyclopaedia Britannica* and then, in 1851, of the novels of Sir Walter Scott for which he paid £27,000. He died in 1874 and his statue is in Princes Street Gardens. The Edinburgh artist, W. Mervyn Glass, lived in this house during the 1960s.

In his day well known as a criminal advocate, Charles Scott lived at No. 9 in the final quarter of the 19th century. A classical scholar of exceptional dedication, he decorated every apartment, other than the basement, in imitation of an ancient Roman house or palace, and it is remarkable that one room has survived in this condition to the present time.

No. 4 Drummond Place is a New Town house with a history of especial interest. Drummond Place was highly esteemed by Sir Robert Lorimer, architect of the National War Memorial at Edinburgh Castle and the Thistle Chapel in St. Giles and the foremost Scottish architect of the early 20th century. His elder, bachelor, brother, John Henry Lorimer (1856–1936), well known as an artist and portrait painter, lived (when he was not staying at the family residence of Kellie Castle in Fife) and had his studio in the house for many years. One of his best-known paintings, executed about 1891 and in the possession of the National Gallery of Scotland, is *The ordination of elders in a Scottish kirk*. For him Sir Robert made a number of alterations to No. 4 (for which permission would not be likely to be given today) which harmonise surprisingly well with the Georgian character of the building. His introduction of curves into the straight lines of panelling on double doors, including the front door, and centrally-placed scrolled plaster ornament immediately above, is visually pleasing, although the heightened mantelpieces enriched with Gothic-style moulded plaster decoration are perhaps less happy. The replacement of window astragals by thick and prominent glazing bars is a successful innovation, but what is to be made of the single, small panel at the top of several doors which has been cut through on three sides so that it can be opened? Possible explanations are that it permitted the circulation of air in winter without the necessity of opening windows or that it provided a draught and thus enabled the fire to burn more readily. These features have fortunately been preserved – although a conservation grant would be available to return the house to its former Georgian state! The Lorimer alterations were carried out by Whytock & Reid.

In the garden, sloping uphill at the back, the original iron posts for securing clothes ropes have survived, as have others in many New Town back gardens, their urn-shaped finials at the top repeating the design of the area railings at the front of the house. A mews lane runs behind the gardens on a higher level, and the coach house that adjoins the stables at No. 4 was adapted to form a chapel, or oratory, for the nuns of St. David's Convent which for some years occupied the houses immediately to the west. Vacated by the nuns in the 1960s, these houses became halls of residence for the Heriot-Watt University, a purpose for which they were no longer required after 1987 when the students removed to the University campus at Riccarton. Though not now in use as a chapel, an 'ecclesiastical' window which had been inserted in the north wall of the mews building looks directly down towards the back of No. 4 Drummond Place across the garden and constitutes an unexpected and delightful feature in the New Town environment.

Another and later painter of eminence to live in this house was Sir William MacTaggart, born in 1903 and a former President of the Royal Scottish Academy, whose home it was from 1938 till his death in 1981. A tablet at the door records his long association with No. 4 together with that of the Norwegian-born Lady MacTaggart. Among the many visitors entertained by them here were King Haakon and the Crown Prince of Norway who later became King Olav. After Sir William's death a sale of his pictures was held in the house which must in many respects have resembled that of Charles Kirkpatrick Sharpe's diverse collections a hundred and thirty years earlier; on that occasion, however, it was held in the premises of the auctioneers. On the days of the MacTaggart sale all the Lorimer double doors were thrown open and the rows of chairs, stretching back through several rooms, which had been provided for prospective purchasers, were filled to capacity.

No. 4 has now been painstakingly restored and refurnished as a private family residence and remains one of the diminishing number of 'grand' New Town houses which still survive undivided (with the exception of the basement which is now a separate flat) into modern times.

In 1953 Nos 31 and 32, which were already joined on two floors, were acquired by Sir Compton Mackenzie (1883–1972), an outstanding Scottish writer of the 20th century, and this remained his Edinburgh home until his death.

An interesting booklet, *The Story of Drummond Place*, was written by one of its residents, Miss Lettice Milne Rae, in 1952. This was updated and reissued in 1970, and a third revised edition was subsequently produced.

Dundas House

This fine classical building is more familiar today as the headquarters of the Royal Bank of Scotland who acquired it by purchase as long ago as 1825 after it had served a period of thirty-eight years as the Excise Office. But it started life, in 1774, as the townhouse of Sir Laurence Dundas, Bart., who represented the City of Edinburgh in Parliament. When the layout of the First New Town was planned it was intended that this prominent site on the east side of St. Andrew Square should be occupied by St. Andrew's Church which would then terminate the eastern vista along George Street as St. George's Church closed it on the west. Sir Laurence, however, was a march ahead of the authorities and feued the ground first for his own residence. It was designed in the new grand manner by Sir William Chambers who went back to ancient Rome by way of the Marble Hill villa at Twickenham for inspiration. The church, thus deprived of its location, had to be built in George Street and many hands were wrung over the aborting of the plans. However unfortunate this may have been, it has to be admitted that Chambers was equal to the occasion and produced an appropriately elegant and stately man-

Dundas House, now the Royal Bank of Scotland, on the east side of St. Andrew Square. The dining-room is now the board-room of the bank.

sion set back within a forecourt which, together with its garden and equestrian statue of the fourth Earl of Hopetoun (added later), still does credit to its environment at the present day. The house has three storeys with four giant Corinthian pilasters framing the windows on the first and second floors, an ornamental frieze below a cornice and a central pediment rising above the roofline.

Chambers (1723–96), born in Gothenburg, Sweden, was the son of John Chambers, a Scottish merchant trading there, and was educated in England. His career began in the Swedish East India Company for which he travelled widely, making sketches of European and even Chinese buildings, but his architectural training commenced in Paris in 1749 and was followed by five years' further study, mainly in Rome. Established in practice by 1755, he lived and worked principally in England. In addition to Dundas House, he designed No. 26 St. Andrew Square about 1770. A balustraded parapet was added to it in 1840 and the north elevation was constructed in 1878.

An incident involving the gambling propensities of the rich and fashionable in the late 18th century links Dundas House to another, no longer there, in the Second New Town. Shortly after its completion Sir Laurence Dundas was playing for high stakes with a practised opponent, General John Scott of Balcomie, who had succeeded Sir George Drummond in possession of the 16th century Drummond Lodge near the village of Broughton. General Scott considered the house to be out of date and inconvenient and did not hesitate to press on when Dundas's pockets had been emptied and it was suggested that Sir Laurence might hazard his new house in a last attempt to redeem his losses. Once more the General outplayed him and the mansion was surrendered. This had, however, taken place in the heat and fervour of the moment, and when calmer counsels prevailed Dundas retained his mansion-house but agreed to pay for the building of another to a similar design to his, thereby satisfying the General's craving for a Georgian stately residence to call his own. The result of this arrangement was the demolition of Provost Drummond's old house and the erection of the new one called Bellevue in its place. By an irony of fate, it also was pulled down less than a hundred years later because of subsidence caused by the building of the Scotland Street railway tunnel (see Drummond Place).

Sir Laurence Dundas was the son of a bankrupt Edinburgh bailie but rose to become a Commissary-General in the Army and by 1762 had acquired both a fortune and a baronetcy. He died in 1781.

In 1725 Alexander Wood, son of a farmer, Mr Wood of Warriston (see Heriot Row), was born in the farmhouse on Wood's Farm. He became well known as a surgeon but was familiarly referred to as 'Lang Sandy Wood'. On his visits to patients he took with him a pet raven and a sheep, the latter being put out to pasture in the garden of Dundas House.

The building which forms the northern side of the Dundas House forecourt was the house, erected in 1769, of the old Scots lawyer Andrew Crosbie, the original of Scott's Counsellor Pleydell in *Guy Mannering* and whose portrait was hung on the walls of the

Parliament Hall. He had lived previously in a long-demolished house in Advocates Close, and Grant records his being 'able to stand his ground in any argument or war of words with Dr Johnson' during the latter's visit to Edinburgh. Andrew Crosbie died in 1784 in impoverished circumstances caused by the failure of a bank in Ayr, and his widow's sole support was a pension granted by the Faculty of Advocates.

After alteration this house became the Douglas Hotel, and it was here that Scott spent the two nights of 9th and 10th July 1832 on his return to Scotland after a vain attempt to restore his health in Italy, as John Gibson Lockhart records in detail in his biography.

Gayfield House

Though now sited within the eastern New Town, Gayfield House was built about 1763 when the northern extension of the city was still on the drawing board. The builders were Charles and William Butter, William being, like Deacon Brodie rather less than a hundred years before, deacon of wrights in addition to being Carpenter to the King. He lived and carried on business in Carrubber's Close in the High Street. Gayfield House is almost contemporary with but smaller than Marionville (q.v.) but now lacks a sufficient amount of open space around it – a disadvantage not shared by the larger house – to be properly seen and appreciated.

Rubble-built and facing south, this most attractive and interesting house has two main storeys, a basement and an attic, the area being sunk to the front but open on both sides and at the back. A Roman Ionic doorway and entablature are reached by a short flight of steps, and the central frontage, consisting of a triangular pediment with urn finials at the apex and each corner above three astragalled windows on the main upper floor and the entrance flanked by two similar windows beneath it, advances slightly beyond the rest of the building which consists of a single bay on either side. A round window in the centre of the pediment lights one of the attic rooms. Gayfield is among the most visually satisfying of Edinburgh's historic houses, and a final flourish is provided by the curved 'Dutch' chimney gables on the east and west sides. Inside is a stair with wooden steps to the basement and the first floor,

Gayfield House in East London Street was built c. 1763 near the old village of Broughton.

while a steep, narrow secondary stair, also of wood, rises to the attic behind a door at first-floor level. The drawing-room on this floor has a coved, carved plaster ceiling and, on the floors of the entrance hall and the first-floor landing is vigorous and well-preserved stencil decoration in black.

The first owner of Gayfield House was Thomas, Lord Erskine, a son of the Earl of Mar who was implicated in the 1715 Jacobite rising, and a later occupant was David, sixth Earl of Leven. In 1767 the *Scots Magazine* carried the report, 'Marriage – June 10. At Gayfield, near Edinburgh, the Earl of Hopetoun to Lady Betty Leven, sister to the Earl of Leven' (see Sylvan Hut).

An unexpected link between the house and the Royal (Dick)

Veterinary College was created in 1874. When the college occupied premises in Clyde Street, now part of the Bus Station to the east of St. Andrew Square, a dispute arose which resulted in the resignation of the Principal, William Williams, at the request of the Committee of Management. Williams decided to set up a rival college and acquired Gayfield House for that purpose. Here he was joined by forty of his pupils, only nine remaining behind at Clyde Street. The venture was wholly successful and lasted until 1904, a period of thirty years. It was during its Veterinary College years that the villa added another interesting curiosity to its original structural and ornamental features. A number of copperplate signatures were cut with a diamond on several panes of glass in the windows of a first-floor room. Anxious, may be, to impress future generations with his achievement, one appears to have been written by the Principal himself and reads, 'W.O. Williams, Esq., M.R.C.V.S., The New Veterinary College, Edinburgh.' 'Professor W. Williams' was also carved but has the appearance of a different hand. On another window could be seen 'John Young, Cockermouth, Cumberland, 1883' and 'J.W. Bennett, Leigh, Lancashire', these last two being probably by

Black stencilled floor decoration in Gayfield House. It may have been carried out in the late 19th or early 20th century and is in a good state of preservation.

students. The panes were later taken out for safe-keeping and are now lost!

When its use as a Veterinary College came to an end the house was bought by a manure merchant, William Cockburn, who remained there until after the end of the First World War.

At some stage in its history the front of the building had been rendered in cement or stucco, and it was some time after it had passed to Messrs. Wallace & McIntyre, Ammonia and Bleach Manufacturers, in 1923 that this was removed, revealing the same beautiful rubble stonework as had been used for the other external walls. The house is of double construction at attic level and it is possible to walk round it in the space between the walls.

Gayfield House stood originally in its own grounds which extended southwards to Leith Walk. In 1790 the land was feued for building by the lawyer James Jollie, the then proprietor, and the resulting Gayfield Square and adjacent streets left the dwelling-house, especially after the construction of East London Street when the villa (as has happened in other parts of the city) became incorporated in that street, with little more than a 'postage stamp' front garden. Its environment was further eroded in 1962 when a telephone exchange was built much too close to the western side of the house. It is still in private, residential occupation and fairly extensive restoration work has been carried out in recent years.

Entered from the north-west end of Gayfield Square is the much later and rather hidden Shaw's Square which takes its name from James Shaw, a house agent who feued the ground and whose office was at No. 6 York Place in the 1870s. There is a strong likelihood that it was built, on the same principle as the 'Colonies' (see Glenogle House), as workmen's dwellings for the builders employed in erecting the streets and houses in the Bellevue area. The house on the corner of Gayfield Street and Gayfield Square but which is also part of the east side of Shaw's Square and which is entered at No. 6 Gayfield Street has marked differences from the other houses in these streets. It is the only one which faces, and is entered from, the west and the only one which is approached by an outside iron stair and a projecting porch which leads into a round hall inside. It may be that this building contains the remnants of a small (possibly farm) house which can be identified on depictions of the area before the building of Gayfield Square and which, greatly altered and heightened, was incorporated in the angle of Gayfield Square and, at a much later date, in part of the enclosing walls of Shaw's Square. The stonework of the streets involved, however, including No. 6 Gayfield Street, appears to be identical.

George Street

'Straight as an arrow flies' was James Grant's description of George Street. He added that, at one hundred and fifteen feet, it was broader than its 'sister streets' and that 'here a great fossil tree was found in 1852.' This was the principal thoroughfare of the First New Town and was built during the 1790s. Many individual buildings have either been replaced or had shop fronts added at a later date, although several have been restored in more recent times and now display their Georgian character to good effect.

Sydney Smith (1771–1845) (see Buccleuch Place), the English wit and divine, as he has been called, stayed in Edinburgh for about six years. Between 1802 and 1803 he lived at No. 46 George Street, having removed there from No. 79 Queen Street. The remainder of his life was spent in London where he achieved fame as a preacher, lecturer and conversationalist.

In No. 60, before the arrival of the shop fronts, the English poet Shelley and his runaway bride, Harriet Westbrook, spent their honeymoon during the month of August in 1811. Harriet was a schoolgirl aged fifteen and her short life ended tragically a few years later when she committed suicide. A plaque commemorating the visit was unveiled outside the building in August 1984, followed by a reading from Shelley's poetry. On a subsequent visit to Edinburgh in 1813 the poet, with his second wife Mary Godwin, and their infant child, stayed at No. 36 North Frederick Street.

Lord Jeffrey (see Buccleuch Place, Queen Street, Bonaly Tower and Craigcrook Castle) lived at No. 92 George Street, having taken up residence there in 1810, for seventeen years.

Great King Street

This was the principal street of the Second New Town, its four palace-fronted blocks being centrally divided by Dundas Street. The end pavilions rise higher by one storey than the rest of the street and were built as single and double flats. Four Ionic pilasters run between the first and second floors in the central projections of this finely proportioned street which was called after George III, designed by Robert Reid and built around 1820.

At No. 3, near the south-east corner, a bronze plaque announces that 'Here Sir J.M. Barrie lodged with Mrs. Edwards, Top Flat, West House, 1879–1882.' Barrie (1860–1937) was at that time a young

A typical New Town Georgian cupola in Great King Street.

journalist embarking on a career which was to lead him, as a playwright, to lasting fame.

Sir Robert Christison (1797–1882), twice President of the Royal College of Physicians, lived at the same address rather earlier than Barrie. He gave medical evidence at a number of trials, the most celebrated being that of Burke and Hare in 1828 when Henry Cockburn (see Charlotte Square and Bonaly Tower) was one of the defending counsel.

The ubiquitous Thomas de Quincey (1785–1859), famous for his opium eating and his articles in *Blackwood's Magazine*, was staying at No. 9 between 1830 and 1834. Of his several addresses, the flat at No. 42 Lothian Street is the one with which he is most often associated in Edinburgh but it is now no longer in existence. He was frequently in debt on account of his inability to deal satisfactorily with his finances and on many occasions sought respite from his creditors by living, with his large family, within the area around Holyrood Palace which afforded sanctuary. His connection with Edinburgh lasted for some thirty years during which time he enjoyed the society of such literary giants of the time as Carlyle and 'Christopher North'. From 1843–54 the de Quinceys stayed in a Georgian cottage at Polton, near Loanhead, where, in the peace and quietness of the country, he prepared the collected edition of his works. This itinerant, eccentric genius died at his house in Lothian Street and was buried in the south-west corner of St. Cuthbert's Churchyard.

Around the year 1830 The Rev. Edward Irving (1792–1834) lived at No. 60 Great King Street. The son of a Dumfriesshire tanner, he turned first to teaching and then to theology, becoming the founder of and the first minister in the Catholic Apostolic Church, after being deprived of office in the Church of Scotland, when his preaching drew large congregations to his services.

Sir William Allan, R.A. (1782–1850), painter and traveller, is commemorated by an inconspicuous plaque at No. 72. He was the second President of the Royal Scottish Academy and was appointed Limner to the Queen in Scotland in 1841. A friend of Scott and a frequent visitor to Abbotsford, it was Sir William Allan who was summoned there by Lockhart shortly before Sir Walter's death to sketch the interior of the house as it was during the occupation of its founder. His portrait of Scott's son still hangs at Abbotsford.

Prior to their removal to Northumberland Street (q.v.), John

A winter scene in Great King Street with the railings of Drummond Place Gardens on the right.

Gibson Lockhart and his wife Sophia Scott stayed in Great King Street, and Sir Walter was writing to them there (without, however, using a street number) in 1820 and 1821. In the latter year he wrote to his daughter on the birth of her eldest son (John Hugh, who died at the age of nine and for whom Scott wrote his *Tales of a Grandfather*), who was therefore most probably born in one of the Great King Street houses.

Heriot Row

The south-facing terrace of the Second New Town, its name recalling George Heriot's Trust who owned so much of the land on which the northern extension was laid out, is a single row of Georgian townhouses with a high-amenity situation opposite the northern side of Queen Street Gardens.

In the year 1857 No. 17 Heriot Row was bought by Thomas Stevenson, the lighthouse engineer, who brought his wife and young son, Robert Louis, up the hill from Inverleith in the hope that the higher and less damp locality would bring an improvement in his health. R.L.S. was then six years of age, and this was to remain his Edinburgh home until 1880 when he, Fanny his wife and, later on, his mother also, went off to the gentler climate of the South Sea Islands. It was here that the future poet and novelist grew to manhood, chose, with less than burning enthusiasm, the law as his profession and spent long nocturnal hours in his garret, as he liked to call it, at the top of the house in early pursuit of his true vocation of writing as, above all, a teller of tales.

From his nursery window the delicate child looked down in the winter evenings as the lamplighter worked his methodical way along the street, leaving behind him yellow pools of gaslight on the pavement. His lively impressions later found expression in the famous lines in *A Child's Garden of Verse*, four of which can be read today engraved on a little brass plate on the iron railings below the lamp:

> For we are very lucky with a lamp before the door,
> And Leerie stops to light it as he lights so many more,
> And O! before you hurry by with ladder and with light,
> O Leerie, see a little child and nod to him to-night!

The house has balconies for plants outside the drawing-room windows on the first floor and, in the early 1870s, the roof of the attic storey was raised to enable the coom-ceilings to be dispensed with. This was done to provide a more comfortable 'garret' for the young writer who so often suffered from seasons of ill-health.

Across the road, in Queen Street Gardens, is the round pond where Louis used to play when the keen east wind gave way to sunshine in the summer. But the pleasure grounds were not always

The doorway at No. 17 Heriot Row, the Edinburgh home of Robert Louis Stevenson, with plaque on the right.

so attractive. After the building of Queen Street this area was little better than waste ground, and even walls and railings were not provided until 1823. Going back still further, the site of Heriot Row lay within the extensive boundaries of Wood's Farm where hares and partridges were fair game to the sportsman and his gun. The old farmhouse belonging to the father of 'Lang' Sandy Wood stood between Queen Street and Heriot Row. The farm extended from Canonmills to the site of Princes Street, then known as Bearford's Parks, and Chambers wrote that in 1824 there were many still alive who could remember the fields 'bearing as fair and rich a crop of wheat as they may now be said to bear houses.' (see Dundas House).

No. 17 was sold in 1894 by the trustees of Thomas Stevenson's estate just six months before the death of his son on the island of Samoa. The house still remains in most respects as the Stevensons knew it (see Pilrig House, Howard Place, Baxter's Place, Colinton Manse and Swanston Cottage).

India Street

In 1819 work got under way in the construction of this New Town street which runs downhill from the west end of Heriot Row to stop abruptly, overhanging Stockbridge, where a flight of stone steps descends to the lower level. It consists mainly of spacious Georgian flats but there are some individual houses as well.

At No. 14 India Street was born James Clerk Maxwell (1831–1879), a neglected Scottish genius whose greatest achievements were in the field of electromagnetic radiation and who has been described as the father of modern science. He numbered the Clerks of Penicuik and Drummond of Hawthornden among his forebears. An outstanding physicist, his first paper was read to the Royal Society in Edinburgh when he was fourteen years of age, and he went on to hold a chair in Aberdeen and subsequently at King's College, London. Having graduated at Cambridge, he returned there later, in 1871, to become the first professor of experimental physics in that university.

Clerk Maxwell was a shy, retiring and deeply religious man who combined the Christian virtues with original thought and brilliant scientific expertise, wholly meriting his favourable comparison with such giants as Einstein and Newton. He died at Cambridge and was buried in his much-loved family estate of Glenlair in Galloway.

North Castle Street

North Castle Street is notable for its architectural detail, including Corinthian pilasters below a triangular pediment and the distinctive bow frontages which project beyond them towards the area railings and the pavement. The most famous of these town-houses is No. 39 which belonged to Sir Walter Scott for twenty-four years until financial misfortune forced him to relinquish it. Grant

The townhouse of Sir Walter Scott, with carved stone tablet, at No. 39 North Castle Street.

calls it 'the most important house in New Edinburgh', and Scott himself wrote in his Journal of 'poor No. 39' on the morning of his departure – the 15th of March 1826. It is on the east side of the street and has in recent years been adversely affected by adjacent new building well out of harmony with the old. Scott's Edinburgh house dates from 1793, and for years a small bust of the Author of Waverley (many of the novels were written here) could be seen behind the front door fanlight (see Atholl Crescent, George Square and Sciennes Hill House).

On the west side of North Castle Street Kenneth Graham (1859–1932) was born in No. 30. From 1898 to 1908 he was Secretary to the Bank of England but is best remembered today for his authorship of books for children, particularly *The Wind in the Willows*, for which he has been said almost to rank with that other great children's writer, Lewis Carroll.

Christopher North's House

'Christopher North' was the name under which Professor John Wilson, appointed to the chair of Moral Philosophy at the University of Edinburgh in 1820, contributed to the august pages of *Blackwood's Magazine*, including his most celebrated work, the *Noctes Ambrosianae*, so called in reference to Ambrose's Tavern in West Register Street, no stone of which remains, in which he and other

Christopher North's house, with oval plaque beside the door, in Gloucester Place.

Edinburgh writers of the first half of the nineteenth century fore-gathered in the joint interests of literature and conviviality. He was a man of striking appearance and animated conversation and combined the qualities, not often found together, of the athlete and the scholar.

From 1825 until his death in 1854 at the age of 69, he lived at No. 6 Gloucester Place near the western end of the Second New Town, a fact recorded on an oval plaque outside the house where the name by which he has been remembered by posterity has been used in preference to his own. Prior to 1825 he had stayed at No. 29 Ann Street. Christopher North's House has been the Christopher North House Hotel for many years (see Abercromby Place, Canaan and Wardie).

Northumberland Street

Northumberland Street, in the Second New Town, was completed in the second decade of the nineteenth century. It was intended to be less grand than its much broader neighbour Great King Street, but grander than Cumberland Street on the other, northern, side of Great King Street. Carved into the stonework beside the door is the public record that No. 25, on the north side, was the residence of Sir Walter Scott's son-in-law and biographer, John Gibson Lockhart (1794–1854) and his wife Sophia from 1823–4. In 1825 they left Edinburgh for London where Lockhart became editor of the *Quarterly Review* (see Great King Street and Portobello).

It was to the family home in Northumberland Street of George Hogarth W.S., that Charles Dickens came to claim his bride. He was a journalist working for the London newspaper the *Morning Chronicle* and first came to Edinburgh in 1834 to cover the granting to Earl Grey of the freedom of the city following the passing of the Reform Bill. Hogarth was an amateur musician who became a composer, violoncellist, and music critic and on his removal to London in 1850 he took up the position of Secretary to the Philharmonic Society. He knew both Scott and Lockhart and other literary figures of the time in Edinburgh.

A 'great public banquet' was given in the Assembly Rooms in 1841 in honour of Charles Dickens at which, says Grant, 'Professor Wilson

presided, and which the novelist subsequently referred to as having
been a source of sincere gratification to him'.

Old Coates House

The oldest house still standing within the limits of the New Town,
built when any extension of the city boundaries was still un-
dreamed of, is the turreted and crowstepped Old Coates, or Easter
Coates, House which displays the date 1615 on a window gablet. It
was built, with strong French influence, in the old Scottish style by
Sir John Byres of Coates, an Edinburgh merchant of substantial
means who had purchased the land in 1610 and whose townhouse
was in Byres Close in the High Street (q.v.). The whole Coates estate

Old Coates House, built many years before the New town was planned, now
stands picturesquely beside its Georgian neighbours.

was originally part of the Barony of Broughton, and Grosvenor Street now occupies the site of West Coates House. The much altered and extended building of Old Coates House bears, in addition to the date of its construction, the initials I.B., M.B. for John Byres and his wife Margaret Barclay of Aberdeenshire. The interior has not survived, but a plaster ceiling on the first floor of the north wing (to which a further extension was added by the Misses Walker of Coates in 1870), with decorative features resembling similar work at Melrose Abbey, still remains. The two sisters built sculpted stones from the Old Town into the stonework, including a window pediment reputedly taken from the French Ambassador's Chapel in the Cowgate.

John Byres of 'Coites', as an inscription on his tombstone in Greyfriars Churchyard states, died, aged 59, in 1629 and the estate passed from his descendants in 1702 when it was bought by the Earl of Rosebery. Approximately two years later it was acquired by the Heriot Trust and was feued by them in 1787 To William Walker (see Dalry House), who gave his name to Walker and William Streets, and who was succeeded by his son, Sir Patrick, who died in 1837 leaving the house and lands to his sisters. None of them had lived in the old house which was occupied by various tenants until 1870. On the death of the surviving sister the Walker estate went in its entirety to the Scottish Episcopal Church for the building of St. Mary's Episcopal Cathedral, and special provision was made for the preservation of Old Coates House which is now used as the Cathedral Music School. The two smaller of the three spires of St. Mary's are known, in commemoration of the two Walker sisters, as the Barbara and Mary spires. It is noteworthy that the Walker tombs are beside those of the Byres family in Greyfriars Churchyard, bringing to an end over three hundred years' connection with Old Coates House and the ancient lands surrounding it.

Old Observatory House

With advice, possibly a sketch, from Robert Adam, James Craig was the architect of Old Observatory House built for an optician called Thomas Short, who also had an interest in astronomy, on Calton Hill. Lack of funds caused delay in the completion of this building, intended to convey the appearance of a fortified house, which was started in 1776 but remained unfinished until 1792 after being taken over by the city authorities. It consists of a round, three-storey tower with a low extension and has pointed, neo-Gothic windows. Crowsteps and battlements decorate the addition of 1893 but Craig's original design was never achieved.

Queen Street

A long row of Georgian townhouses of three storeys and basements, Queen Street was the north-facing terrace of the First New Town. At the time of building it enjoyed an open view of uninterrupted countryside down to the Firth of Forth and across to Fife, and Lord Cockburn recalled, in his *Memorials*, the 'people shuddering when they heard the axes busy in the woods of Bellevue and furious when they saw the bare ground' which was soon to be taken over by the New Town extension builders.

No. 8 Queen Street is notable as being the work of Robert Adam who completed it, with its beautiful plaster ceilings, in 1771 for Chief Baron Orde of the Scottish Exchequer who died six years later. His daughter Elizabeth was the second wife of that formidable old judge, Lord Braxfield, who lived in George Square. It is a daughter of Baron Orde who is credited with writing, in chalk, the words 'St. David Street' on the as yet unnamed side street at the corner house on the south-west side of St. Andrew Square in allusion to David Hume (see James Court) who had just taken up residence there. (Hume's house does not survive but an inconspicuous tablet marks the site on the St. David Street side.) The Baron's house at No. 8, the doorway flanked by double columns and headed by an ornamental frieze, belongs to The Royal College of Physicians next door.

Professor Sir James Young Simpson's is a name still well remembered in Edinburgh. His house, from the year 1845, was No. 52 Queen Street and it was here that his philanthropic, strength-consuming life was based; it was here also that his famous experiments with chloroform were carried out and that his hospitality to both the poor and the privileged was equally and unremittingly dispensed. Simpson himself left an account of his first use of chloroform. He had had the substance beside him for some days but did not have high expectations of its effectiveness. Coming home late one night, his hand 'chanced to fall upon it' and he 'poured some of the fluid into tumblers' in front of himself and his two assistants, Dr Keith and Dr Duncan. 'Before sitting down to supper we all inhaled the fluid, and were all under the mahogany in a trice, to my wife's consternation and alarm'. He was knighted, chiefly for this work, in 1866.

Worn out by his massive labours in many fields of work and study, Sir James, who was born in Bathgate in 1811 and whose mother was of Huguenot descent, died in 1870 at the age of 59 at his house in Queen Street. A portrait medallion was placed in his memory in Westminster Abbey in London, the tomb there which had been proposed being declined by his family. Instead he was buried, beside those of his children who had predeceased him, in Warriston Cemetery (see Strathavon Lodge and Chapel House).

Now known as Simpson House, No. 52 Queen Street belongs to the Church of Scotland.

From 1802 to 1810 Francis Jeffrey (1773–1850) lived in a flat at No. 62. It was during his years in Queen Street that Lord Jeffrey, Lord Advocate at the time of the Scottish Reform Bill and later Member of Parliament for Edinburgh, became the first and most famous editor of that most famous periodical, *The Edinburgh Review* which was launched by him, Lord Brougham and Sydney Smith (see Buccleuch Place). Jeffrey was born in Charles Street, near George Square, and died at No. 24 Moray Place (see Buccleuch Place, George Street and Craigcrook Castle).

Rock House

B uilt on the southern slopes of the Calton Hill, a row of houses now obliquely overlooking Waterloo Place was put up a few years prior to the commencement of the First New Town building programme. The end house on the eastern side, with a tall chimney stack above the east gable, is Rock House which has been associated with successive pioneers in the field of photography since 1843. The first was Robert Adamson who in that year came to Edinburgh and established a studio in the house. In 1844 he took into partnership the artist David Octavius Hill, R.S.A. (1802–70) (see Newington Lodge), who was engaged on a group painting of the Disruption ministers using individual photographs to enable him to achieve accurate likenesses of the many he could not paint in person. Hill and Adamson continued to use Rock House as a studio until the latter's death at the age of 27 in 1848, after which D.O. Hill, celebrated today for his calotypes of Greyfriars Churchyard, Newhaven and other parts of the Edinburgh of his day in addition to his studies of its citizens both famous and unknown, lived and worked in Rock House until his death in 1870.

The next owner was Archibald Burns who also, working with wet plates, produced a photographic record of the city, and he was succeeded in 1880 by Alexander Adam Inglis who continued the photographic tradition. The house was inherited in 1903 by his son, Francis Caird Inglis, A.R.P.S., F.S.A. Scot., photographer to Edward VII and George V, and finally by A.A. Inglis' grandson, also called Alexander Adam, who joined the firm (which had developing and printing works at 15 Meuse Lane, off South St. Andrew Street) in 1929 and who worked in colour and cinematography. After his death the studio was closed and Rock House, which subsequently became a private residence, was sold in 1945 after just over one hundred years as a photographic studio.

Lower down the hill, a short, steep street called Calton Hill running down from the north side of Waterloo Place to Leith Street, contains all that is left of a row of houses built in the second half of the 18th century. In a top flat in the lowest of these houses lived Mrs Maclehose (the 'Clarinda' of Robert Burns) at the time of her famous correspondence with the poet who was then staying in St. James's Square.

Royal Circus

The road to Stockbridge runs through the centre of Royal Circus, quiet and contemplative around its garden of mature trees so that it seems always to be overshadowed by foliage in the summer and autumn. Lying at the western end of the Second New Town, it is architecturally similar but creates an impression entirely different from that of its counterpart at the other end, Drummond Place (q.v.). The architect of this part of the Second New Town was William

Henry Playfair (1790–1857) who also designed the Royal Scottish Academy (then the Royal Institution) and Surgeons' Hall in Nicolson Street. He is buried in the Dean Cemetery where he is commemorated by an inscribed monument.

No. 24 Royal Circus was the home, as its plaque declares, of Sir Henry Duncan Littlejohn, M.D., LL.D., F.R.C.S.Ed (1828–1914), the first Medical Officer of Health for Edinburgh, a position he held from 1862 to 1908. Although he was first in the field in Scotland in that capacity, such an appointment by the Edinburgh Town Council had nevertheless been discussed and delayed on a number of occasions and was long overdue. The event which finally settled the matter was the collapse of one of the High Street tenements which fell, 'storey upon storey to the ground', as Stevenson described it, one November night in 1861. On the 30th of September of the following year, after prolonged public agitation, Dr Littlejohn, at that time Police Surgeon in the city, took up the office which he was to hold for the long and successful period of forty-six years. His task was to sweep away the insanitary conditions of the past, provide better housing for the poor and destitute and instruct the populace in general in higher standards of hygiene and household management. In doing so he laid the foundations of modern public health administration. Referring to the activities of the Health Department during the 19th century, it has been said of Littlejohn that 'there are hardly any aspects of the work of the department over the century in which the hand of Littlejohn is not evident. His knowledge, wisdom and energy became proverbial.' He moved to 24 Royal Circus in 1866 and remained there for the rest of his life.

Royal Terrace Gardens House

W.H. Playfair was the architect responsible for the three Georgian terraces, Royal, Regent and Carlton, in the 1820s. Below Royal Terrace, on land sloping downhill towards London Road, a pleasure ground was laid out with paths and trees for the benefit of the householders in the large terraced townhouses high above it. To accommodate a gardener Playfair himself designed a tiny, pedimented Georgian cottage, standing within its own railed-off garden, in 1836. This fascinating little building is now a private house.

Rutland Street

Rutland Street and Rutland Square, to the immediate west of Princes Street at its junction with Lothian Road, were not part of the First New Town but of its later western extension. The architect was the little-known John Tait who also designed Clarendon Crescent and Eton and Oxford Terraces before his death and burial in the Dean Cemetery in 1856.

In his work here between 1830 and 1840 Tait was in fact completing, and at the same time considerably modifying, plans which had been drawn up in 1819 by a rather more celebrated New Town architect, Archibald Elliot (see Calton Gaol Governor's House). Elliot (1760–1823) was the son of a carrier in Ancrum and began as a joiner, later becoming a cabinetmaker in London. His architectural career is reputed to have commenced when he was taken on as joiner at Douglas Castle in Lanarkshire. A difference of opinion having arisen between the architect and his employer concerning the work being undertaken, Elliot is said to have taken over and completed it himself. In 1794 he began exhibiting architectural designs at the Royal Academy and then worked in partnership with his brother James until the latter's death in 1810. Dividing his time between London and Edinburgh, Archibald Elliot went on to become one of the principal later architects of the New Town designing, *inter alia*, Waterloo Place and the Regent's Bridge. He was buried in the New Calton Cemetery where he is commemorated by a columnar monument.

No. 23 Rutland Street was the place of residence for thirty years of Dr John Brown, still remembered today as the author of *Rab and his Friends* and *Pet Marjorie*. John Brown (1810–82), who practised medicine in Edinburgh and is usually associated more with his literary publications, was the son of an Edinburgh Secession minister, also Dr John Brown, against whom a libel action (in which he was acquitted) was brought in 1845 because of his moderate and liberal views on the Atonement controversy. John Brown, M.D., after leaving No. 51 Albany Street, lived at his Rutland Street address from about 1850 until his death, numbering among his friends such notable men of letters as Ruskin and Thackeray as well as Lords Jeffrey and Cockburn in Scotland. Dr John Brown, Senior, died at Arthur Lodge (q.v.) in 1858 aged 74.

Towards the end of the 19th century the building of the Caledonian Station necessitated the demolition of a large part of the south side of Rutland Street at the Princes Street end to accommodate the new buildings.

24 and 25 St. James's Square

This tenement block on the north side of the otherwise demolished St. James's Square must surely be included among Edinburgh's historic houses. The square was designed by James Craig,

Surviving tenements on the north side of St. James's Square behind the east end of princes Street.

who planned the layout of the First New Town, and Nos. 24 and 25 comprise one of the few remaining examples of his work, his only other surviving building being Old Observatory House (q.v.) on Calton Hill. Apart from his designs for the First New Town, Craig did not become a successful or prolific architect. He died at the early age of fifty-one and is buried in Greyfriars Churchyard where a commemorative stone was placed at the bicentenary of the building of the First New Town which is itself his greatest monument (see Thistle Court).

St. James's Square was built, mainly in the 1780s, to the east of St. Andrew Square and behind the east end of Princes Street on rising ground formerly known as Multrie's Hill but had degenerated to an unreclaimable slum prior to its demolition in 1965 to make way for the notorious St. James Centre. The remaining fragment exemplifies the plain, precipitous nature of the frontages and has strength and dignity even today, while the castle-like appearance of the back elevation with its two curved projections on either side of the high chimney gable gives a massive and towering aspect to these surviving buildings. It is unfortunate that more has not been made of this remnant, still known as St. James's Square, which leads back to the drawing board of James Craig himself.

Robert Burns stayed in the square in 1787 but the house is no longer in existence.

South Charlotte Street

No. 16 South Charlotte Street, at the west end of Craig's First New Town, was the birthplace of Alexander Graham Bell (1847–1922), as recorded at the entrance, Bell having been born in a flat at this address.

At the age of twenty-three he went to Canada and the United States, and his work as Professor of Vocal Physiology at Boston, as well as his study of the techniques of teaching the deaf, resulted, in 1876, in his invention of the telephone. A prototype gramophone was another of his inventions.

Thistle Court

When the first stone came to be laid in the First New Town, the site chosen was Rose Court, now known as Thistle Court, on the northern side of what later became George Street. In the subsequent street design the Court became an adjunct of Thistle Street which, together with Rose Street to the south of George Street, was built as a mews lane (each had a subsidiary lane for stabling behind it) for 'shopkeepers and others'.

The first house in the Court was built in 1767, by a wright called John Young who described it as a tenement, with the characteristics of a country villa. This was an early instance of entrepreneurial risk-taking, in effect a testing of the water, Young having accepted a financial inducement to proceed, and public interest would no doubt be measured by the large crowd which assembled to witness the commencement of building operations. That steps to create the First New Town were taken immediately afterwards can be seen as confirmation that the temperature of the water was considered to be acceptable. Young himself had also feued the ground on which St Andrew's (now St Andrew's and St George's) Church was later (in 1783) built by the Town Council and, to enable the Council to acquire it, they gave him in exchange another area of ground further to the west. Young was, however, in a strong position to lay down certain conditions, one of which was that no provision should be made for burials in or around the new church. He took up a number of other New Town feus as well and served on the Town Council during the 1790s.

John Young, who died in 1801, was described at the time of his important involvement in the construction of the First New Town as an architect, the street which he built in 1780, Young Street, bearing his own name. He was also responsible for the erection of several houses in St. Andrew Square.

It was James Craig himself who laid the foundation stone in Rose Court on 26th October 1767. Two rubble-built semi-detached houses stand at either end facing a narrow garden which runs between them, those on the west side being the plainer and more unpretentious and now containing an electricity sub-station. The warm pink stonework of the eastern houses is enhanced by a pediment over the two centrally-positioned doors, and a lamp on a

Now swamped by modern office buildings, the house on the east side of Thistle Court was the first one to be built in Edinburgh's New Town.

projecting iron bracket above them is an additional feature of distinction which has been preserved. Each house has two storeys and an attic, the latter lit by two dormer windows.

No. 1 Thistle Court was until recently occupied by Mitchell & Baxter, W.S., the legal advisers of Robert Louis Stevenson who was a close friend of Charles Baxter, one of the founding members of the firm.

Thistle Court constitutes the earliest example of New Town architecture.

West Princes Street (No 5A)

The charming little cottage with steeply pitched roof and barge-boarded gables, surrounded by an equally attractive 'cottage' garden enclosed by privet hedges, at the east end of West Princes Street Gardens, was built in 1886 by Robert Morham (1839–1912), the then City Architect, who also designed the Lauriston Place Fire Station (now a fire museum) and the City Hospital. This two-storey, red sandstone gardener's house with the address of No. 5A West Princes Street (but also known as The Cottage, West Princes Street Gardens) is owned by the Edinburgh City Council.

Windsor Street

The name of W.H. Playfair is, more than any other architect, associated with the layout of the eastern New Town around the area of the Calton Hill and the top of Leith Walk. Windsor Street, with an imposing line of Doric-columned doorways, was built as part of this scheme in 1822 in what has been described as a simple but severe Greek style.

In 1827 the actress Harriot Murray, better known as Mrs Henry Siddons, the daughter-in-law of the more famous Sarah Siddons, took up residence at No. 23, having stayed previously at No. 63 York Place and No. 2 Picardy Place. She and her brother, William Murray, the actor and manager of the old Theatre Royal in Shakespeare Square later demolished to make way for the General Post Office, were the grandchildren of John Murray of Broughton who had been Secretary to Prince Charles Edward Stuart. John Murray forfeited his reputation when, having been taken prisoner after the battle of Culloden, he betrayed the royal trust and turned king's evidence against another supporter of the Prince. It was he whose cup was sent flying from a window at 25 George Square (q.v.) by Sir Walter Scott's father, Mr Walter Scott, W.S., after his too inquisitive wife had brought them tea in order to find out who it was her husband was entertaining, Mr Scott declaring that no member of his family would be allowed to drink from it after Mr Murray of Broughton. The 'Secretary Murray' was one of Walter

Scott's clients, and as such he was obliged to speak to him, but their conversation had been strictly confined to matters of business. After this event his youthful son retrieved the undamaged saucer and with it and some other trifles began his collection of curiosities which was later to fill the rooms of Abbotsford and be incorporated in the stonework of its walls.

After Henry Siddons' death Harriot and her brother continued to manage the Theatre Royal but, in spite of apparent success, a sudden financial crisis threatened its closure. The theatre was saved by Scott whose *Rob Roy* had been playing to packed houses in London's Covent Garden. In 1819 it was put on at the Theatre Royal with such immediate success that all outstanding debts were met and the play itself became a national epic. Three years later, when George IV visited Edinburgh, *Rob Roy* was again staged at the theatre, this time by royal command, with William Murray in the part of Captain Thornton.

From 1835 to 1850, in which year he retired at the end of forty years' theatrical work in Edinburgh, William Murray also resided at No. 23 Windsor Street. Fanny, daughter of the English actor Charles Kemble, was a niece of Mrs Henry Siddons and stayed with her in Edinburgh for a few years (see Duncan's Land).

York Place

An eastward extension of Queen Street, York Place was built after the Heriot Trust had feued ground for several streets in that area in the closing years of the 18th century. Sir Henry Raeburn (1756–1823) built No. 32, marked today by his name and dates within an artist's palette on the wall, but as he lived at St. Bernard's, a villa in Stockbridge which is no longer in existence, his large York Place premises do not rank as a historic house. No. 47, however, was the residence of 'the father of the Scottish school of landscape painting', Alexander Naysmith (1758–1840). Here he, his wife (the daughter of Sir James Foulis of Colinton) and their numerous children lived, and here also he gave instruction to his many students. Naysmith, in his youth, had been a pupil of Allan Ramsay (see Ramsay Lodge) before studying in Rome and is supposed to have painted the only authentic portrait of Robert Burns. His son James

(1808–90), inventor of the steam-hammer, was born in the house. Patrick, another son who predeceased him, was at one time as celebrated an artist as his father, and confusion has sometimes arisen in regard to their work, as much of it was unsigned. Alexander Naysmith used his initials on some canvases and, 19th century Scottish paintings currently enjoying a revival of interest, it is significant that the monogram AN has been found to have been added to the work of other painters or to forgeries.

An architecturally unusual house, No. 7, was built in the early 1790s as a rectory for the adjoining St. George's Chapel (since then greatly altered and in commercial occupation), both buildings being the work of Robert Adam's younger brother James. Here is a house that, by combining Gothic and classical architectural detail on an otherwise unremarkable street facade of the period, departs from the Georgian norm of its New Town contemporaries. Of three storeys in height above the basement, miniature battlementing fronts the roof and label mouldings appear above the centre first-floor window and the eastern window on the ground floor, while imitation arrow slits that resemble crosses (and are a reminder of its ecclesiastical origins) flank the centre window on the second. The doorway, beneath a delicate 'lacework' Georgian fanlight, is entered between narrow clustered-column shafts (another feature borrowed from the architecture of the medieval church) and has been placed at the west end instead of centrally, possibly to emphasise the mixing of styles on this interesting and maverick exterior.

Its life as a rectory was short-lived. Within two years it had become a private house in the possession of Alexander Laing. Laing, whose date of birth is uncertain but who died in 1823, started his career as a mason in Edinburgh, styling himself an architect a few years after building the Archers' Hall in Buccleuch Street in 1776 and being admitted to membership of the Royal Company of Archers. The following year he designed the High School of Edinburgh in Infirmary Street to replace the old school building of 1578 on the same site. Sir Walter Scott was a pupil in the Laing building, his enrolment taking place two years after its completion. Between 1786 and 1788 Laing designed and built the South Bridge, but his other diverse achievements were in different parts of Scotland. His house in York Place has been subdivided for many years and used as offices.

'New Town Gothic' can also be found in Albany Street at No. 56. St. Mary's Free Church, built in 1859, was demolished and replaced by offices in 1983. However, 'the neo-Perpendicular Manse at No. 56 survives' (*The Buildings of Scotland: Edinburgh*) on the north side.

Part III
Greater Edinburgh

When the First New Town was built, no need was expected to arise for any future extensions of the city limits. The decision to commence the Second New Town was thought by many to be a reckless and unnecessary venture. But further extensions there were to be, and after 1920 the confines of Greater Edinburgh encompassed no fewer than fifty villages, some of which were in completely rural situations well within living memory at that time. Territorial additions, north and south, were made in the mid-19th century, and in 1896 Portobello, developed as a fashionable Victorian sea-bathing resort, was brought within the town. Granton followed four years later in 1900 along with Restalrig and Duddingston.

But the city was to be enlarged still further by the Edinburgh Boundaries Extension Act of 1920. In that year the Port of Leith (which had had its own Town Council since the Burgh Reform Act of 1833, a period of only eighty-seven years, and which had resolutely opposed the move) was nevertheless included, together with Newhaven and Trinity, as also were Cramond, Corstorphine, Liberton, Gilmerton, Juniper Green and Colinton and the little hamlet of Swanston on the lower slopes of the Pentland Hills which has hardly changed its original character even today.

Open spaces and recreational facilities were not forgotten. In 1884 ninety-eight acres which included Blackford Hill, the first public park to come under the direction of the city, were purchased, and Inverleith Park and the Braid Hills, the latter afterwards devoted to the interests of golf, were both acquired in 1889.

In 1975 yet another act was passed which could be construed as blurring the edges and diminishing the status of Greater Edinburgh. The ancient title of City and Royal Burgh was surely a more becoming designation than that of City and District of Edinburgh within the Local Government area known as Lothian Region into which were now incorporated such previously independent burghs as South Queensferry and Kirkliston. The Regional and District Councils were superseded by Edinburgh City Council in 1996.

Although Edinburgh was already well endowed with houses of historic and architectural significance (a large number of which have been adapted to meet the new and unanticipated requirements of subsequent generations), after the absorptions of 1920 many more were added – farmhouses, country mansions, cottages and even a few buildings which had been used for very different purposes but which (thus introducing a trend in the opposite direction) were turned now into homes and dwellingplaces. It is on these houses lying within the 1920 boundaries, and the people and events connected with them, that attention will be focused in the following pages.

A. North Edinburgh

Ashbrook
Wardieburn

A substantial stone-built, Italianate mansionhouse with a low central tower, Ashbrook, built in 1869, can readily be recognised as an ornate and sumptuous Victorian residence standing behind fresh, green lawns in Ferry Road. It provides a striking architectural contrast to its near neighbour of similar date, Wardieburn House, a little to the west. Wardieburn is in the Scots Baronial tradition with piled-up chimneys and crowstepped gables and has belonged to D.S. Crawford Ltd. for many years.

Ashbrook was the home of Sir Robert Maule, proprietor of Maule's at the west end of Princes Street, a shop which was later equally well known as Binns and then as Frasers. When accounts were paid at Maule's (and other contemporary Princes Street emporiums) the receipt was usually accompanied by a pair of gloves with Sir Robert's compliments! His stately dwellinghouse is now a Salvation Army Social Services Centre for women.

Bangholm Bower

Typical of the early 19th century Trinity villas, Bangholm Bower no longer stands in its original isolation on the north side of Ferry Road near Goldenacre. The tall central block has been separated from its two lower wings to form three houses and, gradually deprived of its surrounding lands, it has suffered the added indignity of being turned back to front. The street of which it has now become a part, Bangholm Bower Avenue, was laid out behind it shortly before the Second World War and the south- facing Georgian frontage looks out over a little back garden and a narrow lane.

The original doorway of Bangholm Bower, an early 19th-century Trinity villa now entered from the other side.

Bangholm Bower is one of many Edinburgh houses to survive into modern times within a completely changed environment and be adapted to meet the needs of a new and more populous age. NEWBANK LODGE, adjacent in South Trinity Road, is the former coach-house of the demolished Rosepark.

Broomfield

The Victorian house of Broomfield belonged to the family of which the First World War field-marshal, Earl Haig, was a member. It stands above the Firth of Forth near Muirhouse, a building with many gables which, with an eastern extension, has functioned for many years as the Commodore Hotel.

Thomas Carlyle's House

In the autumn of 1826 Thomas Carlyle (1795–1881), the great Scottish writer and historian, was married to Jane Welsh of Haddington. Their address for the short period of eighteen months was No. 21 Comely Bank, as recorded on an inscribed stone beneath the central window on the upper floor of this two-storeyed Georgian terraced house.

This area was then a quiet suburb of the city, and the street called, as it still is, Comely Bank led out to Craigleith Quarry. No. 21, says Professor David Masson in an essay on Carlyle's Edinburgh life, was 'the last but two at the outer or country end of the row.' The terraced

Thomas Carlyle's House at No. 21 Comely Bank has a plaque beneath the centre first-floor window.

villas lay 'back a little from the footpath, within railings, each house with its iron gate and little strip of flowergarden in front while' there was 'a larger bit of walled garden behind.' The Carlyles would no doubt be surprised to see how accurate a description that still is today of their early home, but how changed and urbanised is the outlook from its windows.

Caroline Park

Built on the estate of Royston by George Mackenzie, first Viscount Tarbat, in 1685, Caroline Park is a fine example of a Scottish 17th century mansion (although it was referred to as a

The 17th-century mansion of Caroline Park at Granton.

cottage on an inscribed lintel placed above the entrance by its noble builder!) and incorporates the original 16th century Royston House in the central courtyard around which it is built. The south frontage was added in 1696, the projecting portico having an iron balcony above it and the centre block being terminated on either side by imposing, ogival-roofed pavilions. A magnificent wrought-iron staircase and painted wall and ceiling panels adorn the interior, this work, together with two fine panelled plaster ceilings, being of 'great interest as representing the manner in which the baroque flood, rising in the south of Europe, ebbed against the shores of Scotland' (Ian C. Hannah, *Triumphant Classicism* in *The Stones of Scotland*).

The house passed into the possession of the Dukes of Buccleuch in the 18th century and the marriage of Caroline (whose mother had been a maid of honour to George II's Queen Caroline), the daughter of the Duke of Argyle, to the Earl of Dalkeith, the heir to the Buccleuch estates, is believed to explain the name which was given to the mansionhouse.

For many years Caroline Park was occupied by the Printing Ink Factory and Chemical Works of A.B. Fleming and Co. Ltd. who ensured the maintenance and preservation of the house but who moved to larger premises in 1979. It is now in private residential occupation.

It is the great misfortune of this historic mansion, which stands near the sea to the north of West Granton Road, to have survived in a deteriorated and industrialised environment, but the house itself can no doubt be assured of continued protection. One of the well-known occupants in the past was Lady John Scott, the author and composer of *Annie Laurie*.

Challenger Lodge

St. Columba's Hospice in Boswall Road still retains the old name of Challenger Lodge although it was originally known as Wardie Lodge. Designed, probably by W.H. Playfair, in 1825, its pedimented Doric portico dominates the frontage between two large windows, and a cupola surmounts the entrance hall.

This was the home, first of all, of Frances Jane Hope, granddaugh-

Challenger Lodge in Boswall Road was built in 1825 and, after a chequered history, is now St. Columba's Hospice.

ter of the 18th century botanist Dr John Hope, who became a pioneer natural gardener at Wardie Lodge, and later of the naturalist and oceanographer Sir John Murray, K.C.B., F.R.S., who accompanied the Challenger Expedition of 1872–76 around the world for the purpose of drawing up navigation charts. His reports are contained in the fifty volumes which he compiled and edited in the house to which he had given the name of the ship he had sailed in. Sir John died in 1914 and the Lodge later became a home for disabled children. The Hospice, which opened in 1977, has introduced additional buildings in the grounds beside the house and the chapel is one of the chief features of the interior, while the rear windows look out directly across the Firth of Forth.

Craigroyston

Behind spreading lawns and standing back from the sea, at the junction of West Shore Road and Marine Drive, is the mock-castellated mansion of Craigroyston. The two-storey house was built about 1800, its rooftop battlements simulating two square tower heads and its entrance embellished with a 'Gothic' porch. The bay windows are a later insertion, and additions and alterations, including interior plasterwork, were made by Sir Robert Lorimer in 1907. Craigroyston was used as a Naval Headquarters during the War and now belongs to Scottish Gas.

Deanbank House

A small china manufactory was set up 'on the Dean Bank grounds', says James Grant, around 1814, about eight years before the building of Saxe-Coburg Place began. This was a new departure, tanning and milling having been the principal industries in the area. It was, however, unsuccessful, although some pieces of 'Stockbridge China' were preserved in the Industrial Museum, now the Royal Museum of Scotland, in Chambers Street.

When the adjoining streets were laid out, the late 18th century Deanbank House became part of West Claremont Street (now Saxe-Coburg Street) where it joins Deanbank Lane at the southeast corner of Saxe-Coburg Place. This attractive villa has a central block of two storeys with lower wings the end gables of which are obscured on the main (south) facade by walls which extend the frontage and terminate in a ball finial at each side of the building, features which give added character to the house. Chimney stacks rise at each end of the hip-roofed main block, and the house is surrounded by a wall.

The two-storeyed DEANBANK COTTAGE, with a little porch and a large northern extension with bay windows, is round the corner in Deanbank Lane, and close to it is the villa called DEANBANK LODGE. This building, of rather greater consequence than the cottage, is entered through a gateway, the stone pediment of which contains weathered initials, and has been altered by the addition of a third floor. On either side are lower extensions, that on the north being much smaller than its counterpart on the south.

These two houses date from the late 18th century as well and, with Deanbank House itself, form a well-preserved and interesting group.

Drylaw House

Drylaw House, beyond its extensive lawns, stands behind high walls in Groathill Road North. It was built in 1718 by George Loch, a scion of the Lochs of Drylaw who had owned the lands since the middle of the previous century. Their tombs are in Cramond Churchyard where they are designated as being of Wester Drylaw.

The beautiful late 18th-century frontage of Drylaw House.

The architect of the house is unknown but the style has similarities with that of Sir William Bruce, the first exponent of classical design in Scotland.

In the late 1780s it was given a new entrance front on the eastern side. The original doorway, now at the back, is reached by a flight of steps with a curving iron rail. The alterations created a little Georgian mansion of exceptional grace and charm. The door is surmounted by a large, semicircular fanlight and flanked by Roman Doric columns and is contained within a three-bay projection over which extends a triangular pediment above a narrow frieze ornamented with paterae. Two tall chimney stacks rise from the roof-ridge and are complemented by two dormer windows on either side of the projection.

Inside are small, pine-panelled rooms, but the principal feature is the wrought-iron staircase with brass finials.

Duncan's Land

The tenement known as Duncan's Land stands in a lane which used to be called Kirk Loan, as it was the route from Stockbridge to St. Cuthbert's (or the West) Church, and is now known as Gloucester Lane. It is a quaint old edifice built by a merchant called Duncan in the late 1790s beside the Water of Leith with stones brought by him from demolished buildings in the Old Town when Bank Street was being constructed. An ancient lintel, inscribed 'Feare God only, 1605. I.R.', was among them and was built in above one of the doors. The east elevation has a round, projecting stair turret, and the house rises through two floors to an attic with a dormer window on each side of the turret roof. There is a chimney stack above each gable.

On 24th October 1796 David Roberts (1796–1864), the son of a shoemaker, was born in Duncan's Land. While still a child he made drawings on the whitewashed kitchen walls of the house and was eventually apprenticed to a house-painter in West Register Street. Then, says Grant, he 'took to scene-painting, his first essay being for a circus in North College Street; and after travelling about Scotland and England, working alternately as a house and scene painter, he returned to his parents' house in Edinburgh in 1818, and was employed by Jeffrey to decorate with his brush the library at Craig-crook' (q.v.). At this time he was engaged as a scene-painter by William Murray, the Manager of the old Theatre Royal (see Windsor Street).

In 1826 he became scenery painter and designer at Covent Garden and, only four years later, was appointed President of the Society of British Artists, exhibiting frequently at the major London galleries. He was one of the commissioners of the Great Exhibition of 1851. The wide range of his work encompassed paintings exe-cuted in Europe, the Middle East and Africa, though his principal subjects were views of London and the Thames. Many of his pictures were to be seen each year at the Royal Academy and he was made a Royal Academician, the supreme honour, in 1841.

'His parents', Grant records, 'lived to see him in the zenith of his fame', his paintings being sold for 'great prices' (the first time he exhibited had been in Edinburgh in 1822 when he was astonished to sell two Scottish landscapes for two pounds, ten shillings each!).

This celebrated artist buried his parents in the Calton Cemetery, designing the stone himself with the inscription:

> Sacred to the memory of John Roberts, shoemaker in Stockbridge, who died 27th April 1840, aged 86 years; as also his wife, Christian Richie, who died 1st July 1845, aged 86 years . . . This stone is erected to their memory by their only surviving son, David Roberts, Member of the Royal Academy of Arts, London.

Grant describes the abrupt ending of the painter's life: 'David Roberts died suddenly, when engaged on his last work, "St. Paul's from Ludgate Hill". He had left home in perfect health on the 25th of November 1864 to walk, but was seized with apoplexy in Berners Street, and died that evening. He was buried at Norwood. His attach-ment to Edinburgh was strong and deep, and when he returned there he was never weary of wandering among the scenes of his boyhood.'

Duncan's Land was restored in 1974.

Glenogle House

Glenogle House as it now stands was created in 1875, from a smaller earlier building when the Edinburgh Co-operative Building Company erected the Stockbridge Colonies, short terraces of workmen's dwellings which are now of historic interest in their own right. Many of them have the tools of the building trade carved, like miniature trophies, on the south-facing terrace gables. The streets were built between the Water of Leith and Glenogle Road which was then known as Water Lane.

The original name of Glenogle House was Keif House (although it was called Canonmills Cottage on some maps of the area) and was probably put up, in 1780, by the Haig family (see Charlotte Square and Broomfield) whose adjacent distillery (see Heriot Hill House) was constructed in the same year and which has only in fairly recent times been replaced by modern housing.

When the Stockbridge Colonies were built extensions were added on both sides of the house to bring it into line with the other parallel terraces. There are similar 'colonies' in Abbeyhill, Leith and other parts of Edinburgh.

Heriot Hill House

At the corner of Broughton Road and enclosed by a wall that slopes in line with the street leading down to Canonmills is the plain, unpretentious house of Heriot Hill. Erected towards the end of the 18th century, it is built on two floors with small, single-storey wings on either side and has chimney stacks rising to east and west of the central block. In front it retains the statutory round grass plot and carriage drive of the Georgian period.

During the 'meal mob' riots of 1783, when Haig's Distillery at Canonmills (see Charlotte Square, Broomfield and Glenogle House) was threatened with attack as it was thought that oats were being used for distilling instead of to feed the starving poor, a carriage on its way to Heriot Hill House was forced to stop as it was believed that its occupant was a Haig. On discovering that the lady who sat inside, and was considerably alarmed, was of a different family, the mob allowed her to proceed without further hindrance.

The house is now a Royal Navy and Royal Marine Club.

Howard Place

Howard Place was designed in 1807 by the New Town architect James Gillespie Graham (1776–1855) who laid out the Earl of Moray's estate in the western development of the 1820s. His name was originally James Gillespie but, in 1815, when he married the daughter of a Perthshire laird, he 'elongated his surname' to include her maiden name of Graham.

By far the most famous son of Edinburgh to be associated with this plain, Georgian terrace (occupying the east side only of the street) of two-storeys, basements and front gardens was Robert Louis Stevenson (1850–94) who was born at No. 8, a fact which is recorded on a stone tablet beside the door. The delicate Louis spent many a restless night in the devoted care of his nurse, Alison Cunningham – the faithful 'Cummy' of his later as well as his early years. She was engaged in 1851, her previous experience having been gained at Pilrig Manse, not far from the home of Louis's Balfour grandparents, Pilrig House (q.v.).

In 1853 the Stevenson family removed to an exposed corner flat at No. 1 (since 1871, due to later additional building, No. 9) Inverleith Terrace on the opposite side of the street where no diminution was to be hoped for in the prevailing dampness of the district. The previous occupants, the Aytouns (see Abercromby Place), had left for the same reason after just four years, and the Stevensons stayed for exactly the same length of time before their final move to the more healthful climate of Heriot Row (q.v.) (see Pilrig House, Baxter's Place, Colinton Manse and Swanston Cottage).

The poet William Ernest Henley (1849–1903), friend and one-time collaborator of Stevenson, lived 'a few doors from R.L.S.'s birthplace', as Eve Blantyre Simpson, the daughter of Sir James Young Simpson, recorded in her book *The R.L. Stevenson Originals*. The Henleys' only child, Margaret, was born there but died subsequently in London, her 'brief years' having been spent at No. 11 Howard Place. It was during their residence here that Henley was editor of the *Scots Observer*, and here they were visited by Sir J.M. Barrie (see Great King Street) who took a particular interest in the little girl who used artlessly to call him 'Friendy-Wendy', the name he was later to immortalise in *Peter Pan*.

For many years No. 8 Howard Place contained a memorial museum which was open to the public, but the Stevenson relics were removed to Lady Stair's House (q.v.) where they joined those of Burns and Scott in a building now devoted, as The Writers' Museum, to the memory of the three most celebrated names in Scottish literature.

Inverleith House

In 1678 the estate of Inverleith was acquired by Sir James Rochead, or Rocheid, an enigmatic character who, suspected of embezzlement in 1668 while holding the office of Town Clerk of Edinburgh, was dismissed. It has to be said, however, that he was later reinstated although he was also thought to have committed other misdeeds such as endeavouring to influence the outcome of Council elections.

Inverleith House, built in 1773, stands in the Royal Botanic Garden where it served for some years as the Scottish National Gallery of Modern Art.

By the latter part of the 18th century the original house on the estate had become uninhabitable and in 1773 a later Rocheid, also called James, built the present house in what was later to become the Royal Botanic Garden. A severe but impressive building of three storeys with attic and basement on the southern side, it softens on the opposite elevation into a wide, rounded stairtower rising behind a gable-fronted porch, the latter surmounted by a large stone urn and containing the entrance doorway between two windows.

James Rocheid lived with his mother in the new Inverleith House, and they attracted attention on account of their somewhat exaggerated formality of dress and behaviour. Lord Cockburn himself thought Mrs Rocheid of Inverleith worthy of a place in his *Memorials* where her 'peculiar qualities and air' are compared to those of the contemporary actress, Mrs Siddons (see Windsor Street). She rode abroad in a mulberry-coloured coach with 'two respectful liveried footmen', and both the 'coachman and his splendid hammercloth' were 'loaded with lace'. Mrs Rocheid, says Cockburn, 'presided in this imperial style over her son's excellent dinners, with great sense and spirit, almost to the very last day of a prolonged life.'

When the mulberry-coloured coach left Inverleith House it proceeded down a drive which, as Arboretum Avenue, is now a public highway, and, at its junction with St. Bernard's Row, the lodge and gate-piers can still be seen on either side of the road. The gate-posts are crowned by curious stone lions said to have been brought from Edinburgh Castle.

By 1863 the house and grounds were in the hands of the Scottish historian and antiquary Cosmo Innes, but prior to that, in 1820, fourteen acres of the Rocheid estate had been purchased as a permanent site for the Botanic Garden which at that time was located behind Haddington Place at the top of Leith Walk (see Middlefield). Cosmo Innes died in 1874 when the remaining land was bought by the Town Council and added, as an extension, to the Garden. Inverleith House was then used as a residence for the Regius Keepers. In 1960, however, the house took on a new role as the Scottish National Gallery of Modern Art. Although adaptations created suitable and attractive exhibition space, it proved to be too small, and in 1984 the collection was transferred to the former John Watson's School in Belford Road. Exhibitions, usually having some relevance to the Royal Botanic Garden, are, however, still held in the house.

At the eastern entrance to the Garden, No. 8 INVERLEITH ROW

was designed in 1824 for the army surgeon Daniel Ellis by W.H. Playfair to whom he was related. From 1923 to 1973 this house was the manse of the former Broughton Place Church.

The former INVERLEITH MAINS FARMHOUSE can be seen in Inverleith Park and is reached by the path from the East Gate. Probably built in the 18th century, it carries the date 1900 above a doorway, indicating its alteration and modernisation in that year. The original entrance is on the other side.

At the Canonmills end of Warriston Road an unlikely survivor is the little 18th century farm cottage which now finds itself on the edges of late 20th century development. Known as WARRISTON FARM COTTAGE, in the Victorian period it became the gatehouse of Heriothill Station and then the premises of a 'mussel boiler' who left it littered with mussel shells. The building was rescued from dereliction in recent years and used as a pottery, but this was brought to an abrupt end when the site lying between Warriston and Broughton Roads was acquired for house building. The cottage has since been used for a number of non-residential purposes.

No. 52 INVERLEITH ROW was the home of Lt. Gen. William Crockat who guarded Napoleon on St. Helena and who died in the house at an advanced age in 1874, and No. 101, WARRISTON COTTAGE, is an enlarged 18th century cottage, possibly built for a gardener, on the estate of the demolished West Warriston House.

Further to the east, and on the opposite side of the Water of Leith from Warriston Farm Cottage, the former EAST WARRIS-TON HOUSE was converted into the Warriston Crematorium in 1929 by Lorimer & Matthew, the architectural practice of Sir Robert Lorimer. The most recognisable part of the exterior to survive the conversion is the north side. The two-storey house was built in the early 1800s for Andrew Bonar of Ramsay, Bonar & Co., one of the Edinburgh banks whose loans helped to finance the building of the New Town.

Malta House

In Malta Terrace and not far from the Water of Leith is Malta House, its grounds now reduced to the size of a large front garden overlooked by the flats on the opposite side of the street. The two-storey villa with dormer windows, a round-arched doorway and a north-facing Venetian window was built in the late 18th century, although the present roof is the result of Victorian alterations.

The house, which belongs to the Church of Scotland, served for a number of years as a Children's Home. In 1977, however, the children were moved to Clifton Lodge, No. 3 Boswall Road, the Lodge being renamed WALLACE HOUSE in recognition of a bequest from the American-born Dr George C. Wallace, who had never visited Scotland, which financed the purchase of the more suitable building. Malta House is now a Community Care Rehabilitation Centre.

Nearby, in St. Bernard's Row, is the little house called MALTA GREEN. It was built about 1840 and is distinguished by such features, derived from the English Tudor style, as miniature battlementing above a central dormer window and a label moulding above the middle window on the first floor. Malta Green has been restored for residential use.

On the opposite side of the street are two little villas dating from about 1807, ROSEBANK COTTAGE (No. 18) and ST. BERNARD'S COTTAGE (No. 20), the latter subsequently called Glenelg. These plain but attractive rubble-built houses, with their original gardens, are a fortunate survival in an area which still retains many of its original buildings. Another villa, also confusingly called ST. BERNARD'S COTTAGE, stands, within its garden, at the west end of McKenzie Place, a western extension of India Place, close to St. Bernard's Well on the Water of Leith. This secluded, riverside house is of similar date to its namesake in St. Bernard's Row and has had a glazed extension, or porch, added across the entrance.

Mayfield House

A plain, rubble-built villa of the early 19th century, Mayfield House stands on the south side of East Trinity Road. This was the home of Christian Salvesen, a Norwegian who came to Scotland when he was sixteen years old to join a shipbroking firm in Glasgow. Going later to Germany and then back to Norway, he returned in 1851 to set up in business with his brother in the port of Leith, his fleet of whaling ships operating in Greenland and, later, in Antarctic waters. One of his sons became Lord Salvesen, a Senator of the College of Justice, who lived in DEAN PARK HOUSE, beside Daniel Stewart's and Melville Collage in Queensferry Road, which is now the school's boarding house. It was built by the architect F.T. Pilkington in 1874 (see Grange Park and Kingston Grange).

Christian Salvesen died in Mayfield House, aged 83, in 1911. Shortly after the First World War, a gift from his family, it became a home for the orphaned children of sailors, and after the Second World War a Cheshire Home, but was converted into flats in 1998 after the relocation of the Cheshire Home.

In the angle of the two houses of Mayfield and the now demolished Denham Green is EARL HAIG GARDENS, a First World War Settlement for disabled ex-servicemen and their families, built here by the Scottish Veterans' Garden City Association, the land on which it is laid out having been donated by the Salvesen family.

Muirhouse

The estate of Muirhouse, by the Firth of Forth between Granton and Cramond, was purchased in 1776 by the merchant William Davidson who built the original house. This was replaced in 1832 by the present mansion in all its neo-Tudor extravagance. A battlemented tower crowns this building of piled-up 'Gothic' detail in windows, gables, a plethora of ornamental chimneys and an arched doorway at the western end. The east end terminates in a lower, two-storey tower in line with the rest of the house. In the interior the work of the painter Zephania Bell, dating from the 1832 reconstruction, can be seen in the drawing-room.

The founders of the house gave their name to Davidson's Mains (formerly Muttonhole from the sheep that were kept here overnight before being brought into the Edinburgh market next morning), and their descendant, Randall Thomas Davidson (1848–1930), became Chaplain to Queen Victoria in 1878 and, as Archbishop of Canterbury from 1903–28, crowned King George V in 1911. He was born at No. 15 Inverleith Place.

Muirhouse is now used as commercial premises and Muirhouse Mains, across the road, has become a caravan site.

Raeburn House

Of three villas built on land feued from the estate of Sir Henry Raeburn in this area, one has survived and is now the Raeburn House Hotel. Formerly called Somerset Cottage, it was built c. 1832 and consists of a central block with two single-storey wings.

On the south side of Raeburn Place the charming, narrow Raeburn Street with houses on the east side only, was built in 1817 as Hermitage Place. The street was treated as private property with gates at each end which could be locked at night. The gatepiers still remain.

Silvermills House

In West Silvermills Lane, and hidden among the remnants of the old village of Silvermills and the new buildings here of recent years, is the three-storeyed and rubble-walled Silvermills House. Built c. 1760 beside the mill which had been set up when ore from the short-lived silver mine near Linlithgow which had been bought by James VI was brought to the village for refining, it has a good moulded doorway, blocked-up windows on the north gable and has been restored in recent years. The interior, however, has been reconstructed.

The builder of this house was Nicol Somerville, a merchant, who moved to the village of Silvermills as he considered it to be a prosperous industrial community. Originally it had a round grass plot in front of the entrance and was approached by an avenue of ancient elms. As recently as the 1940s there was a farm with cows in Silvermills entered from East Silvermills Lane.

Starbank Park House

In the late 19th century the gardens of the demolished Laverock-bank House and Starbank House, in Trinity, were joined together to create Starbank Park in Laverockbank Road. The latter building

The 'Gothic' doorway of Starbank Park House in Trinity.

was retained as Starbank Park House and stands, in its splendid situation on the raised beach above the Forth, somewhat isolated from its neighbours. This was the home of The Rev. Walter M. Goalan who built the little, tree-sheltered Christ Church in Trinity Road. It was originally a private chapel, the pulpit of which he occupied himself, but later became a Scottish Episcopal church. The congregation was later united with that of St. James' at Goldenacre and the church, with its conical spire and traceried window in a cross-crowned gable, has been converted into a dwellinghouse.

The two-storeyed Starbank Park House, classically symmetrical beneath its far-projecting eaves, has a central doorway surmounted by a 'Gothic' arch and looks south across a rose garden the site of which was occupied by tennis courts at the turn of the century.

The design of this house was used for the smaller LAVEROCK-
BANK COTTAGE at the east end of East Trinity Road, and both were
probably built about the same time in the early 19th century.
Laverockbank Cottage has a round stair-tower with an iron balcony
at the back.

Another house with a similar rear stair-tower is the beautiful East
Trinity Road villa called MARY COTTAGE (but known as St. Marie's
for many years till it reverted recently to its original name) with pear
trees growing on either side of its Ionic-columned doorway. Built in
1823, it has a twenty-feet-deep, stone-lined well fed by an under-
ground streamlet in the garden and is one of several other houses
of great architectural merit built at this time on the north side of
East Trinity Road.

In its York Road garden, at the top of the steep seaward slope, is
the early 19th century single-storey WOODBINE COTTAGE with its

Laverockbank Cottage, in East Trinity Road, is a smaller replica of Starbank
Park House and has a projecting stair tower at the back.

Built in 1823 by George Gunn, a builder probably responsible for other houses of the same period in Trinity, this house has recently reverted to its original name of Mary Cottage and is one of a row of architecturally outstanding villas in East Trinity Road.

intriguing secret hiding-place below the floorboards and the original sewer ventilation shaft beside the gate. Whether it and the demolished Hay Lodge in East Trinity Road (a house of enormous interest which ought to have been preserved) were used for smuggling purposes is never likely to be known.

Strathavon Lodge

O n the west side of Laverockbank Road Sir James Y. Simpson, whose townhouse was No. 52 Queen Street (see Queen Street and Chapel House), built the still extant villa called INVERFORTH for his unmarried sister. Next door, as a country retreat for himself and his family, he purchased Viewbank, an 18th century cottage, which, with his own and later considerable extensions, is now known as Strathavon Lodge. The name was changed because its most illustrious occupant had taken the title of Sir James Young Simpson of Strathavon on receiving a baronetcy in 1866. Here, in the garden, are the stable and coach-house used by Simpson on the occasions when he was able to escape from the exigencies of life in Queen Street for a few quiet days beside the sea, or even an undisturbed night's sleep. There is also a dog 'statue' the original of which is said to have been used in the famous chloroform experiments, but it is probably just a garden ornament as there are others of a similar design in the area.

Further south in Laverockbank Road are the heightened and extended BANKHEAD, formerly Mayville, built as a dower house for the demolished Laverockbank House, WOODVILLE, a charming small Regency villa of c.1811, and IVY LODGE, a two-storey Georgian villa now extended as a nursing home and having a modern cottage and an old well in its garden.

Taap Hall

T aap Hall (No. 219 Ferry Road) stands back within a garden and is a large, plain, seven-bay, stone-built tenement three storeys high with a south-facin frontage. Above the door can be read the name and the date, 1790, when it was put up as the property of a Dutch shipmaster called Thomas Taap.

Trinity Grove

The oldest surviving house in Trinity, built in 1774 by Robert Johnston, an Edinburgh merchant, is TRINITY LODGE at the north-west corner of Stirling Road. Of greater interest, however, is Trinity Grove, dating from 1790 and no longer known by that name. It was erected by David Hunter of Blackness in Angus whose son, Alexander, was a partner in Constable's publishing firm (see Atholl Crescent and Craigcrook Castle) but who died in 1811. The original Trinity Grove was a small, plain, Georgian house but it was soon to be dwarfed by large and more pretentious additions.

Maintaining its literary connection, the next owner was William Creech (1745–1815), Lord Provost of Edinburgh in 1811–13 and a publisher and bookseller at the Luckenbooths in the High Street, who bought it as a summer residence. His townhouse was No. 3 George Street. Concentrating on the garden, Creech made no alterations to the house. He died unmarried in 1815 and Trinity Grove passed to another literary figure (and by far its most flamboyant owner), John Ballantyne (1774–1821), the brother of James Ballantyne, printer and business collaborator of Sir Walter Scott. John Ballantyne was an auctioneer in the city and rode to his auction rooms, says John Gibson Lockhart, 'on a tall milk-white hunter, yclept Old Mortality, attended by a leash or two of greyhounds.' He renamed the house Harmony Hall and covered its walls with portraits of the famous London actresses of the day. Among his guests, who included Constable and Scott, were such celebrities of the stage as Kean, Braham and Kemble who, when appearing in Edinburgh, were usually pleased to avail themselves of his lavish hospitality at Harmony Hall.

John Ballantyne added greatly to the size of the house in 1816 – the long extension of the property to the north, with its little balustraded balcony, its bowed projection and its single-storey section at the northern end which was built, exclusively for his own use, as a private wing. Lockhart writes of how he had the accesses made 'so narrow that it was impossible for the handsome and portly lady who bore his name to force her person through them!' Her husband, however, was small, slight and consumptive, and poor health dictated his early departure from Harmony Hall. John Ballantyne died at the age of 47.

A later owner of Trinity Grove was Sir Richard Mackie, a Leith shipowner who was three times Provost of the port. His signature as ex-Provost heads the list of prominent Leith citizens who protested against the amalgamation of Leith and Edinburgh in 1920, a few years before his death.

In 1927 the house was sub-divided and part of the garden annexed for the building of a western extension of East Trinity Road. Two ornamental storks adorn the roof of the Ballantyne addition on the garden side, and the rather unattractive square tower was a late addition built to take advantage of the northern view over the Firth and, in the opposite direction, to the romantic skyline of the Old Town, as so many Trinity villa-builders had done before.

SHIRLEY LODGE (formerly Primrose Bank House), in nearby Primrose Bank Road, was built about 1750 and has later extensions. It stands within a garden with its south gable towards the street and has high central chimneys above the east front.

Wardie

Often thought to be part of Trinity, Wardie is in fact a district in its own right and has a number of houses which are of historic interest. WARDIE HOUSE in particular, of which only a late fragment now remains tucked away behind Boswall Road, is the most noteworthy. Built originally as Wardie Castle, probably in the early 16th century, it belonged in the 18th century to the Boswalls of Wardie by whom it was rebuilt after becoming ruinous. This 18th century house was reconstructed in 1860 and it is the kitchen premises of that mansionhouse which have survived and still retain the name of Wardie House. An unsuccessful attempt was made in the 1960s to have it demolished as well but, with its crowstepped gable and conically roofed corner turret, both facing out to sea, it still stands beside a diminutive front garden (all that is left of the estate) opposite the western retaining wall of Challenger Lodge (q.v.). Its preservation is fortunate as it now constitutes a little dwellinghouse of considerable charm.

Not far away, at the junction of Granton Road and Wardie Crescent, stands, darkly and heavily ornate, the Victorian residence called GRANTONS, its original corner entrance blocked up and its substantial structure now divided into two separate houses. It was designed by David Bryce (1803–76), the architect of the Royal Infirmary and Fettes College, who incorporated its date of building, 1855, along with other ornamentation into the lintel above the door.

Round the corner towards the sea is LUFRA HOUSE, formerly Lufra Cottage, standing high and looking out across Granton Harbour. Its original corner entrance, too, is no longer used and it now has a more modern approach from Granton View. It was built, as a yachting cottage, by the Duke of Buccleuch who gave it the name of his yacht which had been called after Lufra, one of Sir Walter Scott's dogs.

Returning to Boswall Road, three cottages from the old Wardie House estate are now separate houses entered from the street with their own garden ground in front. The first is EARNOCK, then known as West Cottage. It has a larger garden than the other two and was built in two stages, the oldest part probably dating from the 17th century and the more recent from the latter part of the 19th. SOUTH COTTAGE is a 'but and ben' with an 18th century extension, and the adjoining EAST COTTAGE was the Wardie coachhouse and was once the home of Professor John Wilson (see Christopher North's House, Abercromby Place and Canaan).

Three conjoined houses in Boswall Road are also of interest. The higher standing BOSWALL HOUSE with MANOR HOUSE to the west and WARDIEBANK HOUSE to the east were the property of Sir Donald Pollock, M.D., a former Chancellor of Edinburgh University (see Salisbury Green), who lived in Manor House while the other two became the Pollock Missionary Residences. Wardiebank was originally called Forthview but the name was changed when it and Boswall House were given by Sir Donald to serve as Missionary Residences. The ornamental wrought-iron railings at the street frontage, incorporating the letter 'A' in several places as well as crossed anchors and a trident, were originally part of the interior fittings of the *Aquitania* and were purchased and installed here by Sir Donald, who was a shareholder in the Cunard Line, when the ship was broken up in 1950.

Warriston Crescent

With their backs to the Water of Leith near Canonmills, the quietly elegant two-storeyed facades of Warriston Crescent look out across the open space of the City of Edinburgh Council's Warriston Private Playing Fields. They were built during the first twenty years of the 19th century on part of the lands of West Warriston which had once surrounded the now-demolished mansionhouse of that name on the east side of Inverleith Row. The crescent and adjoining streets were in effect a northern extension of the New Town with which they are in architectural harmony.

In 1848 Fryderyk Chopin (1810–49) stayed with Dr Adam Lyschinski at No. 10 where a plaque was placed on the wall by the Polish community (Chopin was born near Warsaw) in Edinburgh in 1948 to mark the centenary of the visit which had been made during the last concert tour undertaken by the world-famous composer and pianist. He was in Scotland for about three months and during that time he gave a recital in the Hopetoun Rooms in Queen Street, a hall which became incorporated in the Edinburgh Ladies' College which later, as the Mary Erskine School, removed to Ravelston when the buildings at Nos. 68–73 Queen Street were demolished (see Ravelston House). Chopin died the year after his visit and was buried in Paris.

B. East Edinburgh

Bonnington Bank House

In Ferry Road, on the north-east side of the city, Bonnington Bank House has had the good fortune to survive extensive building projects in its vicinity to become the neighbour of Victorian tenements. Distinguished by its architectural features and refinements, this Georgian house with late Victorian extensions which was once the town house of the Earls of Mar and Kellie has a lower western adjunct which served for a time as the Coach House Theatre and was rebuilt when the house was recently adapted as a nursing home. The building was previously used as a Laity Centre by the Roman Catholic Church.

Bonnyhaugh

For years the remnants of Bonnington Village lay in undisturbed deterioration behind Newhaven Road at Bonnington Toll. Only recently has new life come to this once forgotten backwater, although the mill has unfortunately been deemed expendable. The exterior facade of the three-storey millhouse has been retained, including the two narrow windows on either side of the doorway, in front of modern housing, and the old cottages have been restored and modernised. The small mansionhouse of Bonnyhaugh, of three storeys and with triangular pediments above the three third-floor windows, has also been restored and sub-divided for residential use. The rubble-built old house went up in 1621, the Town Council of Edinburgh having undertaken to put a roof over the head of a Dutch dyer, Jeromias van der Heill, who had come to Scotland at their behest to instruct local citizens in his craft.

In the early years of the 18th century Bonnyhaugh became the home of Bishop Robert Keith, a strong Jacobite, who wrote several important works on the Scottish Episcopal Church and who corresponded with Prince Charles Edward Stuart on prevailing ecclesiastical affairs. He died in the house in 1757 and was buried in the Canongate Churchyard.

Adjoining Bonnyhaugh is the single-storey former smithy, with a red-pantiled roof, which has now been transformed into a dwellinghouse.

Unhappily, the old village has been somewhat over-restored, and much of the character has in consequence been drained from these interesting old buildings which form nevertheless an historic group in this somewhat hidden enclave.

Brunstane House

Brunstane is a remote house on the eastern edges of Edinburgh with a stretch of coalmining country between it and Musselburgh. The original building was an L-plan house rather less than a hundred and fifty years old when the great Scottish architect, Sir William Bruce, was summoned fashionably to enlarge it by the Duke of Lauderdale.

Early in the 16th century the mansion, then known as Gilbertoun, was in the possession of John Crichton whose son Alexander was later involved in the conspiracy to bring about the murder of Cardinal Beaton. John Geddie says that the elder Crichton renamed the house after 'his tower on the North Esk above Penicuik' called Brunstane.

In 1593 the lands were alienated to Lady Thirlestane (whose husband had been Chancellor Maitland) and were inherited by her son, the first Earl of Lauderdale (see Queensberry House). His much more famous son, John Maitland, became the Duke of Lauderdale and it was he who married, as his second wife, the notorious Elizabeth Murray, daughter of the Earl of Dysart. She became the sole owner after the death of the unscrupulous and powerful Duke who, as a member of Charles II's Cabal (each letter, ending with l for Lauderdale, being the initial of one of the ministers in that infamous cabinet), had been in a privileged position. As a consequence, when

At the end of Brunstane Road South, on the north-eastern edges of the city, stands the ducal mansion of Brunstane House which was extended in the 17th century by Sir William Bruce. The older tower of the original building is shown here.

it came to the creation of a bigger and better Scottish residence, the King's Architect in Scotland was his to command.

To enlarge the existing structure, Bruce built a somewhat similar tower to the original one at an appropriate distance and linked it to the rest of the building by means of a central addition which contained the new entrance doorway. This work was carried out during the early 1670s.

The interior is noteworthy too – in particular the oak-lined octagonal dining-room and the sash windows which were then an interesting innovation.

The property descended to Lady Lorne, daughter of the Duke of Lauderdale's widow, and through her to the Dukes of Argyle who sold it in 1747 to Andrew Fletcher, a nephew of that stout opponent of the Act of Union which deprived Scotland of her Parliament, Fletcher of Saltoun. As Lord Milton, the younger Andrew Fletcher was Lord Justice Clerk during the Jacobite Rebellion of 1745. He died at Brunstane in 1766.

The last owners to use Brunstane as a family house were the descendants of James, eighth Earl of Abercorn (see Duddingston and Duddingston House), who purchased it from the Fletchers in 1769. In 1875 it was sold by the first Duke of Abercorn to the Benhar Coal Company.

The old house with its long and fascinating history is still in occupation, although some of the adjacent farmland has been sold – another instance of housing needs being met by greenbelt sacrifice.

Stanley Cursiter, the Scottish artist, lived in part of the house in the 1930s.

Cameron House

Overlooking the Queen's Park, Cameron House was built in 1770 by the Dicks of Prestonfield. It is a sturdy Scottish mansion tentatively exhibiting the classical details of the new age in two projecting wings, and with a plain little portico, no doubt added later, in the centre. A small loch in front of the house was afterwards filled in. Like many an ancient pile its adaptability has been proved by its use as a public library for many years and its more recent sub-division into flats. It stands in Cameron House Avenue, off Peffermill Road.

Claremont House

This house, No. 45 Claremont Road, dates from the early 19th century and is one of the Georgian houses, mainly villas (such as Prospect Bank House (q.v.)), which were built on the periphery

Built by the Dicks of Prestonfield in 1770, Cameron House has now been converted into flats.

of Leith Links, most of which have not survived. The single-storey Claremont House has a Roman Doric porch and hides behind a wall.

Craigentinny House

'A little way north-east of Restalrig Village', says James Grant, 'stands the ancient house of Craigentinny, once a simple oblong-shaped mansion, about four storeys in height, with crowstepped gables, and circular turrets; but during the early part of this [19th] century made much more ornate, with many handsome additions, and having a striking aspect – like a Scoto-French château.' The house, which was built in the 16th century and extended and altered in the 17th and 19th, belonged to the Nisbets of Dean and Craigentinny (see Murrayfield House).

In the 18th century, after the long Nisbet ownership, the mansionhouse and its surrounding lands were purchased by a Quaker seed merchant called William Miller. His son, William Henry Miller, was an eccentric character who caused the Greek temple-style monument known as the Craigentinny Marbles to be built off the Portobello Road not far from the old and still occupied farmhouse of WHEATFIELD. The mausoleum, completed in 1856, commemorates his parents and himself and beneath it he was buried at a depth of forty feet in accordance with the terms of his will. Much of this account of W.H. Miller, however, has been refuted by descendants of the Miller family. Although something of a recluse, he appears to have been more normal than he was given credit for, and he was buried at a depth, not of forty feet but of seventeen and a half.

Craigentinny House is now a Community Centre in Loaning Road.

Duddingston

The ancient village of Duddingston, with its Norman church, its loch and its bird sanctuary on the eastern side of Arthur's Seat and the Queen's Park, has preserved its quiet, secluded village character and also many of its 18th century houses. One of the earliest is the two-storeyed and red-pantiled building known as PRINCE CHARLIE'S HOUSE in The Causeway. It was built in 1721 and used for many years as a tavern, and the tablet above the door proclaims it to have been occupied by the Jacobite Prince prior to his victory at the Battle of Prestonpans in 1745. Divided and deteriorated by 1948, the house, of which only the exterior now survives, was bought and restored by the Duddingston Preservation Society.

At the top of its long, narrow and mature garden is the white-painted, two-storey LOCHSIDE COTTAGE. Built in 1787, possibly as a factor's house, by the same Earl of Abercorn (see Brunstane House) who had had the splendid Duddingston House (q.v.) erected for himself about twenty years earlier, it is entered, on the garden side, by a doorway flanked by two narrow windows and has a little 'Gothick'

The exterior of Prince Charlie's House in Duddingston, with a commemorative tablet above the door, has been restored by the Duddingston Preservation Society.

fanlight above which is a small triangular pediment. In 1927 it was sold by the Duke of Abercorn, several alterations being thereafter carried out including the addition of a bow-fronted southern extension, which in no way detracts from its appearance, and the replacement of the old stair by a curving Regency staircase with delicate ironwork and polished, wooden handrail brought from Alderston House in East Lothian. The Adam mantelpieces in drawing- and dining-rooms are 20th century insertions.

DUDDINGSTON MANSE, its most famous occupant being The Rev. John Thomson (1778–1840), the minister of Duddingston Kirk and a noted landscape painter, is in Old Church Lane. It is a large, rubble-built house of the early 19th century, with a doorway at first-floor level approached by a flight of steps. LOCHSIDE HOUSE of c. 1815, and the single-storey CHALFONT ST. ARTHUR, with enormous astragaled windows, are of the same period. The attractive pre-Victorian villa called HAWTHORN BRAE, with a projecting portico, looks down on a sloping garden from its elevated site not far from Prince Charlie's House. It now belongs to the Church of Scotland and is used as a centre for community care.

SOUTHFIELD FARM HOUSE is a well-preserved survivor in Wester Duddingston and at Duddingston Cross Roads the unusual MAYFIELD, built in the years immediately preceding the First World War, is a reproduction L-plan Scottish towerhouse with crowstepped gables and a two-storey turret in the re-entrant angle.

Duddingston House

Duddingston House, off Milton Road West, is one of Edinburgh's finest mansions. It was built in 1768 by the architect of London's Somerset House Sir William Chambers (see Dundas House) for James, eight Earl of Abercorn (see Brunstane House and Duddingston) who had purchased the estate in 1745 from the Duke of Argyle. After enclosing the farmlands, the Earl obtained designs for his new residence and had the park and gardens laid out in the manner of Capability Brown.

Built in an austere classical style, Duddingston House is contained on two floors and, like Dundas House (q.v.), has no basement. The main feature of this stately mansion is the large central pedimented portico supported by four Corinthian columns. A low balustrade runs behind the triangular pediment at the roofline. In keeping with the formal and, indeed, ostentatious spirit of the time, the house was not provided with domestic facilities, the kitchen being located in a separate building which was reached by way of a long corridor or passage. Inside, the magnificent and richly decorated hall rises to the full height of the building, and there is abundance of plasterwork and chimneypiece ornament in the first-floor rooms. In the quadrangle to the north of the house are the stables with a little building in the form of a chapel surmounted by a cupola.

'Prior to the purchase of Sandringham', writes Grant, 'the estate of Duddingston, it is said, would have been purchased by H.R.H. the Prince of Wales, but for some legal difficulties that were in the way.'

Duddingston House, now converted into flats, was built in 1768 by Sir William Chambers for the Earl of Abercorn and is one of Edinburgh's most splendid mansions.

During the Second World War Duddingston House was in military occupation and was subsequently allowed to deteriorate. It was, however, painstakingly restored at a later date when it became the Mansion House Hotel. It has now been converted into flats while the park has been a golf course for many years.

Gibralter House

In the short street called St. Leonard's Bank, on the western extremity of the Queen's Park, stands Gibralter House (No. 12), built in 1782 by Thomas Bridges who had settled in Edinburgh after serving with the garrison at Gibraltar (as it is now spelled). Architecturally it is somewhat similar to Pear Tree House (q.v.) and the name, painted on the gatepost, can still be seen. There are several interesting houses in this little-known street, all of which share the same breathtaking view of Arthur's Seat, Salisbury Crags and the ancient park beside which they have been built.

Hermits and Termits

The strangely-named house of Hermits and Termits stands off St. Leonard's Street not far from the south-western limits of the Queen's Park. It has also been known as David Scott's House and the Coalyard House, both with good reason, but for an explanation of its officially accepted name it is necessary to go back to an early period in Scottish history. The first part probably recalls the medieval monks and hermits of St. Leonard's Chapel and Hospital, of which very little is known, in this area, and the second is derived from the land on which it was built as the word 'termits' may refer to the overseers of a section of farm ground. Hermits and Termits was originally the name of the district in which the house was erected.

Built in 1734 for William Clifton, an Edinburgh Solicitor for Excise, this early Georgian building became engulfed by the station which formed the western terminus of the Edinburgh and Dalkeith Railway, otherwise known as the Innocent Railway, the main purpose of which was the (originally horse-drawn) transport of coal but which also carried passengers – safely, as it happened, hence the name – after 1843. The villa later found itself, situated in a coalyard inside the station gates, put to use as the stationmaster's house. By 1870 the railway was again carrying coal and other merchandise rather than passengers, as the Waverley Station had been opened and the latter transferred to the new suburban line.

The artists David Scott (1806–49) and William Bell Scott lived for a time in Hermits and Termits. David Scott has been described as the greatest imaginative painter of his period, although he was not highly regarded during his short lifetime.

The old railway having reached the end of the line by 1968, the

Once an elegant Georgian villa, the house known as Hermits and Termits in an advanced state of decay in 1972.

house was taken over by Lothian Regional Council under whose auspices it decayed into bricked-up, vandalised dereliction as part of the much-publicised South Side planning blight of the 1960s and '70s. By good fortune it was rescued by the architect, Ben Tindall, who purchased the property in 1980. His restoration of this once more white-walled building with its central chimney gable and original carved panel with a bird above the initials W C M and the date 1734 over the entrance doorway, has brought this fine old building back to life again. The panel was found, broken and damaged, inside the house and has been restored, painted in heraldic colours and replaced in its previous position. Two ram's head stone carvings from West St. Giles Church are built into the outer enclosing wall in front of the house.

The restored Hermits and Termits as it can be seen today.

In the interior Georgian plasterwork and wood panelling were found to have survived in a reasonably good condition, as has the curving mahogany staircase above which the ceiling is ornamented with a clamshell.

Hermits and Termits has been carefully reharled to its 18th century appearance and now serves as office accommodation for the Tindall architectural practice.

Lamb's House

When Mary, Queen of Scots returned to Scotland from France in 1561 she was taken first to the house of Andrew Lamb, a wealthy Leith merchant, to rest after landing at The Shore. The house, however, was rebuilt in the 17th century and, white-harled with steeply pitched roof, crowstepped chimney gables and corbelled stair-tower, stands today as an outstanding example of a merchant's quayside house of this period. Both the architectural style and the internal arrangements (the family living on the lower floors with the warehouse for merchandise at the top) are founded on the ornately gabled merchants' premises that lined the Dutch and Flemish canals, many of which have survived to the present day. It stands in Water's Close, near The Shore, and was presented to The National Trust for Scotland in 1958 by the son of the fourth Marquis of Bute. In association with Edinburgh and Leith Old People's Welfare Council, the Trust restored the exterior of the building, several features from earlier times being preserved inside including an early example of a waste disposal unit in the wall of the stair. Since

Lamb's House in Leith, once the home and warehouse of a merchant in the port, is now owned by the National Trust for Scotland.

1961 it has been used by the Council as a day centre for the elderly.

At the sea end of The Shore Robert Mylne's Signal Tower of 1685, originally a windmill, is another example of an ancient building, erected for quite different purposes, becoming a house in more modern times, several families being accommodated in the case of the Signal Tower. Also in this category and in the same area is the Cooperage (No. 5 Commercial Wharf), a large, gable-ended, waterside building of five floors and attics. Built in 1840 as a cooperage and a derelict building for many years, it has now been restored and remodelled as flats. The Vaults at No. 87 Giles Street, a rubble-built, 17th century warehouse with 18th century alterations, has also been restored and developed for a similar purpose. Part of the building, which is entered through a cobbled courtyard, may date from the 16th century, and it was occupied by Cromwell's troops in 1649. Eighteen flats were constructed within The Vaults in 1984.

A number of other Victorian bonds and warehouses in Leith have now been similarly adapted for residential occupation.

Lochend House

The best view of Lochend House is from the park across the waters of the ancient Lochend Loch where only the 16th century fragment of the old fortified dwelling of the Logans of Restalrig (see Gogar Castle) is visible. The rubble walls have two windows, and above rises a chimney stack of massive and conspicuous proportions.

The Logans were the old superiors, to its detriment, of Leith, and the last baron, Sir Robert (as most of them were named), played a notorious part in the Gowrie Conspiracy during the reign of James VI. With him came to an end the long Logan line and an end also to the intrigues and stratagems of this lawless race who clung tenaciously to the old feudal ways when the Middle Ages were passing into history and the day of the manor house was bringing domestic amenity, with its inevitable changes, to the keep and the towerhouse.

In the early 19th century a substantial villa was built alongside the remnant of the older building, and this is used as a day nursery for children.

A memorial window designed by Sadie F. McLellan to the Logans of Restalrig was installed and dedicated in Restalrig Parish Church in October 1984. It was donated by their American descendants to mark the sexcentenary of the succession of that family to the lands of Restalrig in 1382.

Louisfield

The name of this east-facing, two-storeyed house, built c. 1810, on the south-west corner of Willowbrae Road, with a twin-columned entrance portico and slightly projecting pavilion wings on the north and south ends of the main frontage, is taken from its builder, a Frenchman called Louis Cauvin. His father, also Louis Cauvin, came to Edinburgh in the 18th century where, after teaching French for some time, he became a small tenant farmer at Jock's Lodge, and it was here that he died in 1778. His son also taught French in the city until 1818 when he too turned to farming, renting a large acreage in Duddingston called Woodlands and building the elegant villa of Louisfield which was enlarged after his death in 1824 to form Cauvin's Hospital for the founding of which he left an endowment and instructions that it should be used for the mainte-nance of twenty boys, sons of teachers and farmers, whom failing of respectable printers and booksellers. The hospital was opened in 1833 and was administered by trustees including the Lord Provost, the Principal of Edinburgh University and several local ministers.

Cauvin, one of whose pupils for a short time was Robert Burns, and his parents are buried in Restalrig Churchyard, and the Cauvin Trust was amalgamated with the Dean Orphanage in 1929.

Louisfield has now been adapted as residential flats for the elderly.

Marionville

The mid-18th century house of Marionville (see Gayfield House) still stands beside the road that bears its name, but its plain, unassuming exterior hides an exuberant and colourful history. When newly erected it was known as 'Lappet Ha'' in derisive reference to two industrious sisters whose millinery shop within a High Street close had enabled them to build it with the fruits of honest labour and no doubt a native frugality as well. From these sturdy and independent origins the house entered a picturesque and flamboyant era on being acquired by Captain James Macrae of the 6th Dragoon Guards, who was a cousin of the Earl of Glencairn, the patron of Burns, and had married the daughter of the Swedish ambassador.

He and his family being 'gay and fashionable', as Robert Chambers, who tells the story in some detail, called them, the house became the scene of amateur theatrical productions of which many notices appeared in the Edinburgh newspapers. When visiting his wife's cousin in Paris, the private theatricals they saw at her elegant house in the *Marais* were soon being used as 'the models of those afterwards instituted at Marionville' where the character parts were taken by themselves and their friends.

Captain Macrae possessed, however, 'a temper which was apt to make him commit actions of which he afterwards bitterly repented', and on a spring evening in 1790 a dispute arose between him and Sir George Ramsay of Banff concerning which of them had prior claim to a sedan chair at the end of a performance they had been attending in the old Theatre Royal. This minor incident became exaggerated into a quarrel the outcome of which was finally decided by a duel between the two men. Sir George being unfortunately killed, the Captain, in great distress, fled the country, ending his days in Paris in 1820 and never daring, throughout thirty years, to return to his home and sorrowing family. Marionville, no longer the centre of fashionable amusement, acquired, says Chambers, 'an air of depression and melancholy such as could scarcely fail to strike the most unobservant passenger.'

The house is a large and monumental villa of two storeys, a basement and an attic and, with its single dormer window like an outlook for the banished wanderer's return, it outlives its melodramatic past with dignity. In 1929 St. Ninian's Roman Catholic Church was built in the grounds and Marionville is now preserved and used as the church house.

Middlefield

Sited now behind Leith Walk between McDonald Road and Pilrig Street, this attractive but run-down Georgian villa no doubt indicates by its name what its original situation was like when it was built in 1793. Middlefield has three storeys, a pilastered doorway below a pedimented centre window, which is itself between two 'Gothic'-glazed Venetian windows, at first floor level, and a gabled attic floor.

Further down Leith Walk, on the same side and near the corner of Springfield Street, is the little sunk building known as SPRING-FIELD COTTAGE. It is a survivor from the early days when Leith

Middlefield, a country villa built in 1793 and now obscured by the tenements of Leith Walk.

Walk, or Leith Loan as it was then called, was first built on the line of General Leslie's defensive rampart thrown up between Leith and the Calton Hill for the purpose of driving back the invading Cromwellian army in 1650. The earthwork eventually became the principal road to Leith and houses began to appear along its length. They were built on the level of both the rampart and the corresponding trench which was eighteen feet below it. At Springfield Cottage a flight of steps at the west side leads down from the pavement to the house, which has been in commercial occupation for many years, and a wooden paling, now replaced by a more substantial barrier, was put up to prevent the possible descent of unsuspecting pedestrians to the lower level. To distinguish the upper from the lower

The gardener's house of the former Physic Garden in Haddington Place with stair to 'Low Walk' level. It has now been altered by the introduction of a concrete 'flyover' entrance from the street to the upper floor.

line of houses, this arrangement was known as the High Walk and the Low Walk, the latter having all but disappeared.

One other example remains. In the upper part of Leith Walk, at Haddington Place, can be seen the last relic of the old Physic Garden that was moved to that site from the area of the present Waverley Station, along with the separate physic garden at Holyrood, in 1763. This is the Low Walk-level, two-storey, rubble-built house below No. 34 Haddington Place. It was built as the GARDENER'S HOUSE by the Keeper, Dr John Hope (1725–86), for John Williamson, the first gardener, and stood at the entrance to the Garden. The Linnaeus monument (a modified Robert Adam design), now in the Royal Botanic Garden at Inverleith (see Inverleith House), was also commissioned by Dr Hope and was originally set up, in 1779, at the Leith Walk garden. An interesting exhibition entitled *Our Place*, showing details of this area, was held in McDonald Road Library in March 1986 by the Gayfield Association.

Nairne Lodge

Originally called Caroline Cottage, Nairne Lodge stands in Willowbrae Road, not far from Duddingston Cross Roads, and was built in the opening years of the 19th century. It is a simple, two-storey building with the main, east-facing frontage terminating in projecting bows at either end.

This was the home of Carolina Oliphant (1766–1845) of the Jacobite family of Gask in Perthshire where she was born. In 1806, at the age of forty, she married her cousin, Major William Murray Nairne, and lived for a short time in Portobello. Moving to the cottage, they changed its name to Nairne Lodge and it was here that their son, a delicate child who was never to experience good health, was born in 1808.

The Oliphant lands and the estate and title of the Nairnes had been alienated after the 1745 Jacobite Rebellion and, both being reinstated by George IV, she was thereafter known as Lady Nairne. Lord Nairne died in 1830 and, on the death of her son seven years later, she left Edinburgh, eventually returning to and dying in her native Gask. She wrote, or re-worked, many well-known Scottish songs, including *The Laird o' Cockpen, The Land o' the Leal, Farewell to*

Edinburgh and *Charlie is my Darling*, but, as she kept their authorship a closely guarded secret, it was not until after her death that their true attribution was revealed by her sister, Mrs Keith.

Nairne Lodge later became a hotel and has suffered from alteration and extension.

Norton Villa

Stranded in a drying green behind Easter Road on the eastern side is the sole survivor of a row of 18th century houses. Known as Norton Villa, it has a somewhat Victorian appearance with bay windows, probably later additions, on both floors on one side and a central, bargeboarded porch, and takes its name from the nearby Norton Place, called after an Englishman, the Hon. Fletcher Norton. The son of Lord Grantley of Yorkshire, he came to Edinburgh after the Jacobite Rebellion of 1745 and was appointed a Baron of the Scottish Exchequer in 1776. With his Scottish wife and family he lived in a house which once stood on the site of the station at Abbeyhill. Norton Villa is still occupied as a family home.

Peffermill House

A house of rather dark and frowning aspect, half hidden among trees, Peffermill (or, more anciently, Peffermiln) was built in 1636 as a three-storeyed, L-plan structure with a stair-tower in the re-entrant angle, steeply pitched roofs, crowstepped gables and gableted dormer windows. It was also known as Paper Milne, coarse paper being made here in the late 18th century. There was also a bleachfield for thread. Constructed for Edward Edgar of the Wedderlie family in Berwickshire, it stands near the Braid Burn, a situation which no doubt accounts for its name, Peffermill, in Anglo-Saxon, meaning 'the mill on the dark muddy stream'. John Geddie mentions a tradition that the house was connected by a subterranean passage with Craigmillar Castle (q.v.) on its eminence to the south, but the distance between the two would have rendered this a formidable undertaking.

The splendid 17th-century Peffermill House from the west.

Sir Walter Scott, writing *The Heart of Midlothian* in the garden of Duddingston Manse (q.v.), could look directly across the loch to the gaunt old mansionhouse, and it is said to be the original of the residence of the Laird of Dumbiedykes.

Many changes have in recent years overtaken Peffermill. A new road runs between it and its old neighbour the Braid Burn and modern housing has gone up within a stone's throw of its ancient walls. In the 1930s it was the home of the architect A.F. Balfour Paul whose works include St. George's School, the First World War Memorial in Donaldson's Hospital (now Donaldson's College) and the Sir William Fraser Homes in Spylaw Bank Road. The Fraser Homes were built in 1898, a year or two after the cottages at Coltbridge (not by Balfour Paul), these two very different architectural conceptions being based on the same almshouse principle with donor's tablets on the walls (see Coltbridge House). Peffermill was restored in the early 1980s.

Pilrig House

Although the interior of this fine old house on the east side of Pilrig Street has vanished, it must nevertheless be included among Edinburgh's historic dwellingplaces. It has, however, been rebuilt as flats, largely with the original stones, faithfully copying its old appearance and is a reminder to all who see it of its past history as well as its present place in the community.

Pilrig House in 1968 with the sundial on the left.

Pilrig House was built in 1638 for a goldsmith called Gilbert Kirkwood, but the lands had previously been in the possession of the family of Monypenny, lairds of Pilrig, or, as it was anciently known from a peel tower in this area, Peelrig. The L-plan 1638 building was of harled rubble and may have incorporated part of an earlier house. The doorway, approached by a flight of steps, had columns with a frieze and cornice above added at a later date, but all the original architectural features were situated at the top – dormer windows, with the date of building, ornamented by crescents and fleurs-de-lys and a curving gable above the entrance containing a round attic window below a tall central chimney stack.

The house is now best remembered for its association with the Balfours who first came to Pilrig in 1718. It was bought in that year by James Balfour whose father, also called James, had had a ship-building yard in North Leith and who is said to have died of a broken heart after sustaining heavy losses in the disastrous Darien expedition. The Treaty of Union between Scotland and England of 1707, however, had made provision for the repayment of the capital which had been invested, together with interest, and by 1718 James's son

Pilrig House in 1974 after the interior had been destroyed by fire.

Pilrig House rebuilt as flats in 1986.

was in a position to purchase the Pilrig estate with, as John Russell, the Leith historian, has described it, 'its mansion and park, meadows and cornfields and silvery stream of Broughton Burn.' As a result of that purchase the house subsequently acquired its association with Robert Louis Balfour Stevenson whose maternal grandfather, The Rev. Lewis Balfour (later minister of Colinton Church and occupant of its manse (q.v.)), was born here in 1777.

The Balfour tenure lasted until 1941 when, on the death of Miss Margaret Balfour-Melville, the house passed, in terms of her bequest, to the Corporation of the City of Edinburgh who had already obtained over twenty acres of the Pilrig estate for the creation of a public park for the citizens of Leith. The mansion and its garden were taken over with civic ceremony and a sundial, with the dates 1718–1941, was placed on the front of the building at the west side to mark its long Balfour period. It is unfortunate that from the latter date the slow decline of Pilrig House can be clearly traced.

In spite of an undertaking to preserve the fabric and to use the historic building for appropriate purposes, Pilrig House was allowed by the authorities to fall into disrepair, and after serving as a Civil Defence centre, a boy's club and a firemen's hostel, ten homeless families were given emergency accommodation within its twelve rooms in 1946. By 1954 it was empty except for a caretaker who was forced to leave in 1969 due to the penetration of the roof by rainwater and general deterioration. Decaying property in a public park becomes, sooner rather than later, a target for vandalism. In 1971, therefore, and again the following year, the roof with all its architectural detail was destroyed by fire and the house reduced to a gutted and ruinous shell.

Many suggestions had been made at intervals as to how best to resuscitate the old house, but no action was taken until, in 1985, life was brought back at the eleventh hour by the creation, including a replica turnpike stair, of six flats within the restored exterior walls, the opening ceremony being attended by several descendants of the Balfour family.

Presenting once more its familiar profile to the outside world, the regeneration of Pilrig House has taken place at a time when Leith itself is being revived and revitalised, after many years of neglect, with new building, new industry and new hope for the future (see Baxter's Place, Howard Place, Heriot Row, Colinton Manse and Swanston Cottage).

Portobello

The eastern suburb (until 1896 the Parliamentary burgh) of Portobello grew gradually, from small beginnings, on the Figgate Muir across which, out of Duddingston Loch, the Figgate Burn winds its way towards the sea. It takes its name from the West Indian port which was the scene of a British victory over the Spanish in 1739. An old Scottish seaman who had served in the campaign returned to Edinburgh and settled in the area where he built, in 1742, a thatched cottage, long since vanished, to which he gave the name of Portobello Hut.

Some twenty years later, in 1765, a deposit of clay was found near the Figgate Burn by William Jamieson who set up a tile and brick works, followed by an earthenware manufactory, which resulted in an increased population and the building of houses. By the opening

The eccentric Portobello Tower was built as a late 18th-century villa for an Edinburgh lawyer.

years of the 19th century ground had been feued and the first streets were being laid out which, together with the invitingly sandy beach that bordered the little town, drew attention to its suitability as a bathing resort for the people of Edinburgh who wished to indulge in the newly fashionable activity of sea-bathing. Many of the Georgian houses of this period still survive, a number of them sadly (and badly) in need of renovation. Jamieson himself went into villa building also, but only one of his houses – and that a most eccentric one – has stood the test of time. This is an extravaganza called PORTOBELLO TOWER near the west end of the Promenade. Built in reddish-coloured brick, it consists of an octagonal, battlemented tower attached to which is a similar but square stair-turret. Frag-

All that remains of Shrubmount, the last home of Hugh Miller, in Portobello.

ments of other buildings, including parts of the old Mercat Cross of Edinburgh, are incorporated copiously in the fabric of this 'villa' which was constructed for a lawyer, John Cunningham, who had feued the ground from Jamieson, in 1785.

Attractive Regency houses are to be found in such streets as Brighton Place and Crescent, Regent Street and Adelphi Place. In Melville Street (now Bellfield Street) Sir Walter Scott visited his daughter and son-in-law at No. 37, and it was in this terraced house, with its white-painted doorway and dormer window and little front garden, that Lockhart (see Great King Street and Northumberland Street) wrote part of his biography of Scott.

At No. 3 BRIDGE STREET is the single-storey, whitewashed and pantile-roofed little cottage where, as recorded on a tablet on the wall, Sir Harry Lauder was born in 1870, although reservations have been expressed about the exact location of his birthplace.

The late Victorian period is well represented towards the eastern end of Portobello by such buildings as the imposing, red stone Windsor Mansions and the bay-windowed flats of St. James's Terrace. In Windsor Place, and opposite the now demolished early 19th century Windsor Place Lodge, is WINDSOR HOUSE, an unusual

Beside the road at the eastern extremity of Joppa can be found the white walls and brick chimneys of Rock Cottage, a survivor from the days of the salt works at Joppa Pans.

villa of c. 1860 with prominent Gothic-style glazing, partially coloured, in every window, the lower ones Gothic-arched, and in the fanlight above the door.

Picturesquely situated by the Figgate Burn are the old red-brick, gabled houses of the brickmakers with white-painted window openings and an air of quiet resignation in the face of a lost industry. The potteries have gone as well, leaving two kilns behind them as nostalgic street decoration.

A house in Portobello High Street which has become incorporated into a row of tenements contains the only remaining remnants of SHRUBMOUNT, a two-storeyed Georgian villa which was the last home of Hugh Miller (1802–56), the stonemason from Cromarty

Georgian architecture in Brighton Place, Portobello.

who became a world-famous geologist and author. Overwork, concern for the safety of his fossil collection in the museum he had created at Shrubmount and other anxieties drove him to shoot himself within his house at the age of 54.

Shrubmount had an extensive garden and its entrance portico faced south towards Figgate Street (now Tower Street). On the ground floor inside the present-day tenement, on the left-hand side, can be seen the two columns of the portico, virtually all that is left of the original house.

Joppa, eastwards of Portobello, also has good examples of houses dating from the late 18th century.

Formerly part of Joppa Salt Pans, ROCK COTTAGE, at Joppa Pans, is a fairly large 18th century, gable-ended house of two storeys with tall brick chimney stalks rising from the pitched and pantiled roof which has small, brown-painted urns at either end. This five-bedroomed house has a walled garden on the sea side at the back. The salt works at Joppa Pans were well known in the 19th century and the Scottish Salt Company Limited was situated there in the 1930s.

Queen's Bay Lodge

In 1890 Charles Jenner, of Jenners department store in Princes Street, built the house known as Queen's Bay Lodge in Milton Road, Easter Duddingston. It is a long, rambling building, the central part, on two floors, having a tall chimney stack rising between two steeply pitched and red-tiled gabled roofs.

The principal feature is the design of the enclosing railings on Milton Road. Running beneath them is the explanatory inscription: 'The Scaliger Railing "Verona" 1380. This exact copy was made at Portobello Midlothian 1890 by James Ross, Blacksmith, along with David Greig, his assistant in the work.' The main motif of a ladder (from the Italian *scala*) framed by ornamental ironwork is repeated throughout the design, the original railings enclosing the tombs of the Scaliger family in Verona.

The house is now a Church of Scotland Residential Home for the elderly.

On the opposite side of Milton Road the former MILTON HOUSE is now the King's Manor Hotel.

Restalrig

In the Middle Ages Restalrig was bigger and of greater importance than Leith, and it was not until the late 15th century, when St. Mary's, the forerunner of the present Parish Church of South Leith, was built for them, that the population of the emerging port was spared the long walk to what was then the large and famous Restalrig Church.

Today the old main street of Restalrig is part of Restalrig Road South and contains a few houses of age and interest. The oldest is the WRIGHT'S HOUSE, No. 62, its gable having a single window looking towards Restalrig Church on the other side of the road. The date 1678 is incised on the lintel of the moulded doorway at the side. Directly opposite the church, their doors now blocked up, the street frontages of a row of old cottages have been used to provide the outside wall of Restalrig Church Hall.

The old Wright's House in Restalrig with a lintel dated 1678 on that part of the gable wall which does not face the street.

Beyond the Wright's House on the other side and opposite the entrance to Loaning Road is the house called BROOKLYN (No. 75), an early 19th century villa altered and extended about 1880. Like Portobello Tower (q.v.), it is said to have older ornamental stonework from demolished buildings built into its walls, and its squat, round, battlemented tower rising centrally behind a pointed, deep-roofed gable and another gable with a central chimney stack, is a somewhat incongruous feature of this unusual house which has a projecting crowstepped porch at the entrance inside the garden. Next door at No. 77 is BROOKLYN COTTAGE, a small, Georgian, cottage-style house from the first half of the 19th

Brooklyn House – an unusual building dating from the early 19th century in Restalrig.

century with massive, white-painted outside shutters at the windows.

St. Ann's Bank House

A rubble-built house of considerable charm surrounded by old walls and trees and with an entrance flanked by gate-piers with ball finials is St. Ann's Bank House, No. 17 Spring Gardens. It has a high chimney gable containing windows in the centre of the main frontage, a Roman Doric doorway and looks south across the Queen's Park.

St. Ninian's Manse

St. Ninian's, the original North Leith Church and Manse, was built in 1493 (in what is now Quayside Street) beside the first bridge to be built across the Water of Leith. The church was reconstructed as a four-storey warehouse in the early 19th century and in more recent times the manse was incorporated in the Quayside Mills of McGregor & Co. (Leith) Ltd., animal feedstuffs manufacturers. The buildings here, which had suffered serious deterioration, are currently in course of restoration by the Conservation Trust of The Cockburn Association who state that 'The north part of the St. Ninian's Manse is early 17th century with the ogee belfry added in 1675', the north part being in use as a tenement by the mid-18th century. The belfry is of wooden construction and is crowned by a lead-covered spire. 'The southern part of the building is early 18th century.'

When the new Georgian North Leith Church was built in Madeira Street in 1816 the old church and manse were sold to a shipbuilder when the Manse was described as 'containing a parlour, drawing-room, four bedrooms, kitchen, storeroom, brewhouse and vaulted cellar.' A garden lay 'between the harbour and the church'. It is intended by the Cockburn Conservation Trust that the restored Manse should be used as an office.

Salisbury Green
St. Leonard's
Abden House

Salisbury Green, on the east side of Dalkeith Road, stands behind walls and entrance gates and was built in the second half of the 18th century by Alexander Scott, an Edinburgh merchant. At that time it was a country house well to the south of the city boundaries.

Salisbury Green was purchased by the Dicks of Prestonfield (see Prestonfield House) and after the death of Sir Alexander Dick in 1785 his second wife, who was a niece of the biographer

James Boswell, took up residence here together with her children.

Many alterations were made to the old house when it was acquired, in 1860, by the Edinburgh publisher William Nelson whose family home it was to remain for the next thirty years. Turrets, gargoyles and other features inspired by the towerhouses of 16th-century Scotland transformed the building into a Scots Baronial mansion with two additional wings, the architect being John Lessels who also designed the now demolished Nelson's Parkside Printing Works. The gardens were laid out with a terraced lawn sloping to the south and east to capture the long views of Arthur's Seat and Duddingston Loch.

Beside Salisbury Green is St. Leonard's which was also designed by Lessels and built in 1869 for William Nelson's son Thomas. A

St. Leonard's is a mid-Victorian house which was built for Thomas Nelson, the Edinburgh publisher.

huge, baronial composition with piled-up turrets, oriels and gables with an equally impressive and ornate interior, the massive four-storey tower supports above it a strange little attic building said to have been used by Nelson as a 'cottage', presumably on the occasions when he grew tired of the grandiosities of his pretentious residence.

Abden House, built in 1855 and of little architectural merit, was given to Edinburgh University together with Salisbury Green and St. Leonard's by Sir Donald Pollock, a former Chancellor of Edinburgh University. Abden House was used as the official residence of the Principal of the University and the Pollock Halls of Residence were built in the grounds of the other two houses. Sir Donald lived in Manor House in Boswall Road (q.v.).

Outside the Pollock Halls complex is MARCHHALL, built in 1854, which is now a nursing home.

The hamlet of St. Leonard's, with its chapel, is first mentioned in the records of the 13th century.

Seacote House

A little Regency villa, now divided into four flats, eastward of Leith Links beside Seafield Avenue, Seacote House was built about 1820. Rediscovered by the Cockburn Association in the 1970s, it is a plain, two-storeyed building with chimneys confined to the gable-head on either side and stands at the end of a short drive entered by gate-piers.

Nearby, No. 16 Prospect Bank Road, built originally as PROSPECT BANK HOUSE, is another example of the survival of a Georgian house, dating in this instance from the end of the 18th century, to become part of a much later street. This white-walled house of two storeys with single-storey wings has several blocked-up windows and is entered across a narrow basement (See Claremont House).

To the east of both these houses, and situated now at the entrance to the Eastern General Hospital at Seafield, is FILLYSIDE HOUSE with a good Ionic-columned doorway on the west-facing main facade. The ground here was once known as Phillside and was part of the lands of Coatfield.

Prospect Bank House, a late 18th century building surviving as No. 16 Prospect Bank Road.

Smith's Place

On the east side of Leith Walk, between Lorne and Manderston Streets, is the little side-street of Smith's Place. Closing it at the further end is the fine Georgian villa also called Smith's Place. Built in 1812 by James Smith, a merchant, who also laid out the street, it has a central projection containing a doorway with a good semicircular fanlight, at ground level, a pedimented attic window with urns at each end on the apex of the pediment, and a Venetian window above the basement on each side of the projection. There are entrance steps and area railings at the front and the arrangement of the chimneys, which rise decisively above each of the three pediment urns, gives strength and cohesion to the architectural composition.

The house has belonged for many years to Raimes, Clark & Co. Ltd., wholesale chemists.

Victoria Park House

Originally known as Bonnington Park House, the much-altered and extended Victoria Park House was built in 1789. Facing south and entered from Newhaven Road, it looks beyond the tree-planted lawn to Victoria Park, a public recreation area with a statue of Edward VII overlooking Newhaven Road. It has bay windows on the west side of the main facade and a tall, round-headed window in the gableted western addition.

This house went out of private occupation in 1918 when it was purchased by the city and has since then been run as a day nursery for children. This use was temporarily interrupted when it was taken over as an isolation unit during the smallpox epidemic of 1942.

The single-storey lodge was also built in 1789 but has a modern flat roof.

C. South Edinburgh

Arthur Lodge

A neo-Greek villa of great charm and originality on the corner of Blacket Place and Dalkeith Road, Arthur Lodge (originally Salisbury Cottage) was built in 1830, probably by the Greek Revival architect Thomas Hamilton (1784–1858), for the jeweller William Cunningham. The villa stands in a garden and is bounded by high walls on the eastern side. Restrained Greek motifs are incised as decoration on the main facade, a 'Grecian' statue stands in a shallow, rounded recess at the east end of the south, or garden, front, and the principal feature of the interior is the atrium and staircase with short, rotund Ionic-column balusters. Mural wall and ceiling paintings have been added in some rooms in recent years.

John Brown, D.D., minister of the Secession church in Rose Street and then of its daughter church of Broughton Place, lived at No. 10 Gayfield Square before his final removal to Arthur Lodge where he died, aged 74, in 1858 (see Rutland Street).

The house was subsequently the residence of the early 20th century artist W.G. Burn-Murdoch in the possession of whose family it remained for many years.

Arthur Lodge lies on the north-east edge of the Blacket estate, first developed in the early 19th century, with its splendid stone-built villas and later Victorian houses. Some of the streets here were originally closed by gates during the hours of darkness and the gate-piers can still be seen, while three lodges also remain in Dalkeith Road. The intention was to provide for the residents of these streets the privacy more usually associated with a country house. The Blacket area was designed in 1825 by the New Town architect James Gillespie Graham.

In Blacket Place is the Doric-porticoed BLACKET HOUSE, its coach-house now a separate dwelling, and at No. 38 Mayfield Terrace, with ornamental carving above its portico, can be found

Arthur Lodge, a Greek Revival villa of 1829 beside Dalkeith Road.

NEWINGTON LODGE, one of the earliest houses in the district and the home of the pioneer photographer D.O. Hill (see Rock House) during the last years of his life. NEWINGTON COTTAGE, No. 15 Blacket Place, has a pediment above its Tuscan portico. In the same street, and in contrast with the classical elegance of these buildings, are the florid, Victorian houses on the opposite side, No. 60 having gables with tall finials at the top. BELLEVILLE LODGE, built c. 1835 (No. 5 Blacket Avenue) has a large garden where 'a cow was kept in the 1880s until milkmaids were no longer available from Newington.' It is now a nursing home.

Bank House

Formerly known as Morningside Bank, Bank House is situated, facing south, at the top of a steep embankment on the west side of Morningside Road near Churchhill and was built in 1790. It stands crowstep-gable-ended to the street below, and the gablets of two semi-dormer windows, which can be seen above the pinnacled roof of the conservatory, are crowstepped too, as are the other gables, one of them bay-windowed, on the west side of the facade. Chimneys are carried by the gable apex at either end of the house.

This was the boyhood home of Dr Cosmo Gordon Lang, Archbishop of Canterbury from 1928 to 1942, and his brother, The Very Rev. Dr Marshall B. Lang, when their father, The Very Rev. John Marshall Lang, later Principal of Aberdeen University, was minister of Morningside Parish Church from 1868–73. The Archbishop, Lord Lang of Lambeth, wrote of his vivid memories of the church 'as well as of Bank House, whose garden was a great joy to us children.'

Bank House was divided into Middle Bank House and North Bank House about 1860.

Borthwick Of Crookston's House

With its back to Lauriston Place and its Georgian frontage looking south on to St. Catherine's Convent to which it belongs, is the sole survivor of the villas erected in this area in the 18th century. Built by William Borthwick of Crookston in 1770, it was known in the mid-19th century as Lauriston Lodge.

Dr Boswell's House

In a letter to Dr Johnson written in 1777 James Boswell, his future biographer, tells him that he has 'taken the little country house at which you visited my uncle', Dr Boswell. There was a garden of three-quarters of an acre with fruit trees and flowers, and the view from the study window included Arthur's Seat. No other information was given from which the location of the house could be discovered, and it was the Edinburgh historian, the late W. Forbes Gray, who traced Dr Boswell to No. 15a Meadow Place in Marchmont. The house and its environs have seen many changes and the building now stands behind high walls in a narrow lane. In 1881 it was altered and extended to form two separate houses (see Boswell's Court and James Court).

Bruntsfield House

'The massive, ancient and dark edifice, with small windows and crowstepped gables', as James Grant describes Bruntsfield

Built on the Burgh Muir, Bruntsfield House belonged to the Warrender family from 1695 to 1901 and is now part of James Gillespie's School.

House, was built on the Burgh Muir by the Lauder family in the late 16th century. In 1603 it passed from them to the Fairlies of Braid (see Comiston House and Hermitage of Braid) and then, from 1695 until 1901, it was held continuously by the Warrenders, commencing with George (later Sir George) Warrender of Lochend, merchant, Lord Provost of Edinburgh in the reigns of William III, Queen Anne and George I, and subsequently Member of Parliament for the city.

In the 18th century two large and inappropriate windows were inserted in the high, sheer walls of a 17th century extension which are totally out of sympathy with the earlier 'small windows' mentioned by Grant.

The Warrenders were the last owners to use Bruntsfield House as a family home. Escaping demolition as streets of tenements went up around it, the old pile, carefully restored, became incorporated in the early 1960s in a complex of modern buildings to form the new premises of James Gillespie's High School, thus ensuring the preservation and maintenance of one of Edinburgh's oldest and most interesting houses for the foreseeable future.

Buccleuch Place

In 1801 Francis Jeffrey (see Queen Street, George Street and Craigcrook Castle) brought his bride to No. 18 Buccleuch Place. Here in the third-floor flat they occupied, Jeffrey, Sydney Smith and Henry Brougham conceived the idea of commencing a literary magazine which was realised the following year and which was to have far-reaching influence as *The Edinburgh Review*.

Sydney Smith was a Church of England clergyman who preached on occasion in Charlotte Chapel at the west end of Rose Street. He was a close friend of Jeffrey and also of Cockburn and, on his own admission, left Edinburgh with 'great heaviness of heart' in 1803 (see George Street).

Lord Brougham (1778–1868), who became Lord Chancellor of Great Britain during his brilliant legal career, was born at No. 21 St. Andrew Square where a plaque on the wall can still be read. Henry Peter Brougham was active in the cause of Parliamentary Reform and the abolition of slavery.

A plain Georgian street on the south side of the city, Buccleuch

Place was built in the 1770s by James Brown, the architect of the
adjacent by George Square (q.v.).

Burghmuirhead House

Isolated behind the Baptist Church on the west side of Morningside
Road stands the large, gable-ended Burghmuirhead House, the last
remaining building of the old village of that name which, as it suggests,
lay at the head of the Burgh Muir. It was surrounded by gardens,
difficult to imagine now in its present car-park environment, and for
many years was called Grangebank. In the early 19th century the
house belonged to Thomas Steel, a surgeon and member of a local
family of doctors and chemists (who gave his name to Steel's Place
nearby), but by 1850 the Steels were no longer in possession.

A subsequent owner of Grangebank was John Bartholomew who
died there in 1861. It was a later member of this family of cartogra-
phers who lived in Falcon Hall and who, on its demolition in 1909,
removed part of the facade and had it re-erected as the frontage of
the Edinburgh Geographical Institute in Duncan Street which has
now been converted into flats. The gates along with two stone
falcons were placed at the entrance to the Edinburgh Zoo (see
Corstorphine Hill House).

In 1892 Grangebank became St. Theresa's Orphanage for Girls
and then, until 1914, a Roman Catholic school. The house was
purchased by Lodge Abbotsford in 1920 and the old structure, the
plain appearance of which belies its 17th century origins, was
extensively renovated. Further repairs were carried out in 1955.

The village of Burghmuirhead was laid out on the lands of
Greenhill, and a stone panel (designed by George Washington
Browne, the architect of the residential property built subsequently
on its site) on the corner of Bruntsfield Place and Bruntsfield
Gardens is carved with a representation of the demolished Greenhill House. This four-storey mansion had belonged to the Living-
stons of Greenhill. A tombstone commemorating John Livingston,
a victim of the 1645 outbreak of plague in Edinburgh, is in a walled
enclosure at No. 1 Chamberlain Road.

A similar but smaller and less ornamental panel can be seen at
Nos. 43/45 Springvalley Terrace depicting the now vanished

Springvalley House, at one time the home of James Grant, the author of *Old and New Edinburgh*.

Canaan

An area of land in the Morningside district was known as Little Egypt as long ago as the late 16th century, and the name of Canaan appears to have been introduced to designate adjoining ground to the north in Covenanting times when the use of Biblical names was common practice. Between Canaan and Jordan Lanes lay the tiny neighbourhood of Paradise, its gardens becoming known, in local parlance, as 'the kailyards of Paradise'. Goshen, immediately to the east and even smaller, has one surviving house surrounded on all sides by later building but still occupied and still called GOSHEN HOUSE.

Several mansionhouses, together with their grounds, were taken over by the Astley-Ainslie Institution (now Hospital) and opened in 1923 as a convalescent hospital attached to the Royal Infirmary of Edinburgh. Some of these houses, notably Millbank, have been demolished but several 19th century residences, such as ST. ROQUE and MORELANDS, are preserved and in use as part of the hospital buildings.

CANAAN LODGE, later St. Andrew's Priory, is outside the hospital grounds and stands in Canaan Lane. Built in 1800, the house and its five acres of ground were purchased in 1814 by James Gregory (1753–1821), Professor of Medicine at the University of Edinburgh and still remembered today for 'the famous mixture which bears his name'. He had been born in Aberdeen (his mother was a daughter of the thirteenth Lord Forbes), and his portrait by Raeburn and his large medical library were bequeathed to Fyvie Castle, the library being presented to Aberdeen University at a later date. Canaan Lodge was rebuilt in 1907 and the last owner died in 1937.

Also in Canaan Lane is WOODVILLE (no. 49), the home of James Wilson, F.R.S.E. (1795–1856), the brother of Professor John Wilson (see Abercromby Place, Christopher North's House and Wardie), who settled here on his marriage in 1824. He was the author, among other books, of the natural history articles in the seventh edition of the *Encyclopaedia Britannica*, all of which were written at his 'charming retreat', as it is called by his biographer, 'of two acres, snugly ensconced amidst the groves of Morningside.'

The large CANAAN GROVE, now a pavilion for adjoining tennis courts, is in Newbattle Terrace. In Jordan Lane is JORDAN BANK VILLA, No. 15, which was bought in 1867 by Sam Bough, R.S.A., the landscape painter, and in Eden Lane, a quaint and attractive backwater, stand HARMONY HOUSE, EDEN VILLA and some cottages.

The Jordan Burn flows past the Astley-Ainslie grounds on their southern side towards Blackford where the old Blackford House was demolished to make way for Blackford Hill branch line railway station, the station having also, in its turn, disappeared, at the foot of Blackford Avenue. The rubble-built, two-storey BLACKFORD FARMHOUSE survived here for long in a derelict condition but has now been rescued and converted to meet present-day housing requirements. The chimneys have been removed and skylight windows inserted in the roof.

Chapel House

Chapel House is a somewhat forlorn survivor in a changing and much changed environment near George Square. Standing in Chapel Street, it was built in the mid-18th century and has had the unusual experience of witnessing the disappearance of its ground floor. It is approached through gate-piers beyond which a carriage drive originally sloped downwards to the house, but the earth became built up during the course of time to such an extent that the lower storey was obscured beneath it. The building was ornamented with a parapet and stone urns at the roofline.

In 1840 this interesting house was acquired by the Edinburgh tea merchant Andrew Melrose (see Easter Park), whose household included thirty apprentices as well as his own family. On his death in 1855 it became a maternity hospital administered by trustees one of whom was Sir James Y. Simpson (see Queen Street and Strathavon Lodge).

The interior of Chapel House has been destroyed and the building, appropriately reconstructed, now serves the Pakistani community in Edinburgh, a mosque having now been built behind the retaining wall.

Nearby in Forrest Hill, off Forrest Road, is one of several examples to be found in Edinburgh of an old building becoming a house, or, as in this case, flats, in the 20th century. In this short street the north side of the large and otherwise demolished Charity Workhouse, built in 1743, now serves a rather different residential purpose!

Clinton House

Near East Morningside House (q.v.) is the large, bay-windowed and bargeboarded Clinton House, erected in 1876 in a style resembling that of the Victorian architect David Bryce. This was the home, built by her when she was seventy years of age, of the widow of Lt. Gen. James Kerr Ross who had seen service under Wellington. She could remember Waterloo and, at the age of ninety-one, wrote a military march in honour of Queen Victoria's Diamond Jubilee in 1897 which the Queen was pleased to accept. At one hundred and two she purchased a new grand piano on which she practised a little every day until she died, at one hundred and three, in 1909.

The house has been subjected to very few alterations and still retains its original conservatory at the western side.

Comiston House

Entered from Camus Avenue, Comiston House is a little classical mansionhouse of great charm and character. Replacing an older house, it was built in 1815 for Sir James Forrest, Lord Provost of Edinburgh when Queen Victoria visited the city for the first time after her coronation in 1842. Some fragments of the original house still remain. The lands of Comiston belonged to the Fairlies of Braid (see Bruntsfield House and Hermitage of Braid) but the first house was built by Andrew Creich who left his and his wife's initials and the date 1610 on a dormer window which was later built into another building.

The present house, for many years an hotel, has twin columns on either side of the entrance, giant pilasters at the east and west corners, a central pediment above the middle window of the first

Comiston House after restoration in 1996.

floor and a half-sunk basement. After the closure of the hotel it was boarded up and derelict for a number of years until restored as flats and the ground around it landscaped in 1996.

Craigmillar Castle

Although it is not known by whom it was first built, on the walls of the ruined and high-standing Craigmillar Castle on the southern edges of the city can be found many traces of its owners for nearly three centuries, commencing in 1374 when it was owned by the Prestons of Craigmillar. Their arms, three unicorns' heads, and their rebus, a 'press' and a 'tun', are visible in many places throughout this historic building. The Preston Aisle in St. Giles commemorates their gift, which became its principal relic, of an arm bone of the saint. 'A later scion', says Geddie, 'was that Sir Simon Preston, Provost of Edinburgh, in whose house in the High Street Mary, a prisoner after Carberry Hill – the wooded height in full view of Craigmillar – spent her last night in her capital.'

The square, central keep, its walls as much as nine feet thick, is surrounded by a curtain wall with flanking towers and machicola-

Craigmillar Castle, a substantial ruin with a long history, was a favourite country residence of Mary, Queen of Scots.

tions from which it and other buildings in the enclosure could be defended. The great stone-vaulted Hall, thirty-six feet in length, has a fireplace eleven feet wide, and above it is the 'little chamber, only seven feet by five', called Queen Mary's Bedroom. The other buildings are of later and varying dates, the most recent being the west range put up as a family mansion about 1661 by Sir John Gilmour whose family removed later to The Inch (q.v.). The castle was at one time surrounded by a deep moat and bears the Royal Arms, which could mean that it was regarded as belonging to the king in time of war.

The history of Craigmillar is closely linked with the house of Stuart. In 1517 the young King James V was taken there to escape the pestilence, and in 1544 the castle was captured by the Earl of Hertford by whom it was plundered, sacked and burned. Rising again, rebuilt, from this destruction, it became a favourite resort of Mary, Queen of Scots. She sought solace here after Rizzio's murder and again after that of Darnley when she was soon followed to Craigmillar by the Earl of Bothwell.

Surviving the storms of history into a placid and dignified old age, the castle is an outstanding and prominently situated medieval ruin of which more could be made as as attraction for visitors by the City of Edinburgh.

The Drum

One of the most famous of Edinburgh's great houses is The Drum at Gilmerton (q.v.), built in the 1730s to designs by William Adam for the thirteenth Lord Somerville. Originally known as Somerville House, William Adam's work here, which has had many critics, is strongly influenced by the Palladian architects of 17th century England and, indeed, remains incomplete as the eastern pavilion was never built. The house incorporates an earlier

The Drum, an ornate Palladian mansion at Gilmerton, was built by William Adam in the early 18th century.

The house of Drumbank, built in the 1840s, echoes the Georgian period at the beginning of the Victorian on the city's southern limits.

building of 1629 which had itself replaced a previous house of 1585 by John Mylne, one of the earliest of the long line of Master Masons to the King in Scotland.

The heavily rusticated central block is dominated by a huge Venetian window on the upper floor over which a pediment, containing the Somerville coat-of-arms, thrusts upwards into the line of the roof balustrade, with its ornamental urns, immediately above. A horseshoe stone stair carries the entrance over the basement area.

The interior of The Drum is characterised by rich and beautiful if somewhat extravagant plasterwork, much of which was probably executed by Thomas Clayton, while the curving staircase is a calm and graceful feature of this exuberant building. The grounds were laid out by William Adam and the stable block was built in the early years of the 19th century. It has belonged to the More Nisbet family for many years.

In Old Dalkeith Road, on the north-east periphery of the Drum estate, is DRUMBANK, built in the 1840s and echoing the style of the Georgian period. This is an interesting house as it demonstrates the transition from Georgian elegance to the heavy and ponderous designs of the Victorian era. Drumbank stands on the Edinburgh side of Danderhall but is just outside the 1920 city boundary.

East Morningside House

The large, white-harled East Morningside House, built by the merchant Gavin Baillie in 1726, was originally a secluded mansion standing within grounds that stretched from Whitehouse Loan to Morningside Road. A two-storeyed, dormer-windowed building with a west wing, now a separate house, added in 1850, it has suffered from too many alterations and adaptations at different periods and is unusual in possessing a square, north-facing 17th century doocot with over two hundred nesting holes, a fifteen-foot-deep well, and a willow tree said to have been grown from a cutting taken from Napoleon's garden at Longwood on St. Helena. The doocot has been converted into a small dwellinghouse.

In 1801 the house was purchased by James Ferrier, W.S., Principal Clerk of Session and a colleague of Sir Walter Scott, and it was here that one of his ten children, the Edinburgh-born novelist Susan Edmondston Ferrier (1782–1854), authoress of *Marriage, The Inheritance* and *Destiny*, lived when not at her New Town residence in Nelson Street which she acquired after her father's death in the Morningside house in 1829. The Ferrier family home had previously been at No. 25 George Street where Burns, Scott and Mrs Piozzi, the friend of Dr Johnson, were frequent visitors.

James Grant describes Susan Ferrier as 'one who may with truth be called the last of the literary galaxy which adorned Edinburgh when Scott wrote, Jeffrey criticised, and the wit of Wilson flowed into the *Noctes*.' She died unmarried at the age of seventy-two.

The Elms
Elm Cottage

A turreted, baronial house with large crowstepped gables in Whitehouse Loan, The Elms was built in 1858 and is now a Church of Scotland home for the elderly. Elm Cottage, opposite The Elms in Blackford Road, has been converted into two houses. It was once the home of the Edinburgh historian Sir Daniel Wilson (1816–92) and his brother George Wilson, M.D., F.R.S.E. (1818–59). George Wilson was the founder of the Industrial Museum which in 1861 became the Royal Scottish Museum, and Sir Daniel wrote the history of the city, *Memorials of Edinburgh in the Olden Time*, during the 1840s. Later he went to Canada in search of further material for the museum which was sent home by the Hudson's Bay Company. He died in Canada in 1892.

George Square

About 1763 'a sagacious builder, by name James Brown', says Robert Chambers in his *Traditions of Edinburgh*, '. . . purchased a field near the town for £1200, and feued it out for a square.' This was the site of what James Grant calls 'the massive suburban mansion', known as Ross House, which was the residence of the Lords Ross of Halkhead and which, 'with the fields and gardens lying around it', consisted of about twenty-four acres. A large quadrangle of 'neat houses' having been erected thereon it was given the name of George Square after George Brown, the builder's elder brother, Ross House having been sacrificed to provide the first classically-designed square in Edinburgh a few years before the commencement of the New Town.

From the middle of the 20th century onwards this enclave, which is still the largest square in Edinburgh, was steadily eroded by demolition and the erection of high-rise University of Edinburgh buildings, all attempts to preserve the square being disregarded. Only the houses on the west side of the central garden remain unscathed, and it is fortunate that No. 25 has therefore lived to tell its tale in stone of the part it played in the saga of the life of Scott (see Atholl Crescent, North Castle Street and Sciennes Hill House).

In 1772 the 'stern old Edinburgh lawyer', as John Geddie calls the elder Walter Scott, 'left the purlieus of the Old College' for George Square where it was hoped that 'the better air of this new district' would be more favourable to the health of 'his growing and weakly son' who was then just one year old and who, apart from the time he spent in the Border country, was to remain here until his marriage in 1797. From this house each Sunday Mr and Mrs Scott, with their children and domestic servants, walked from George Square to their pew in Old Greyfriars Church and 'no doubt visits were paid to the family burying-plot, where Scott the elder is now laid, near the entrance to the Heriot grounds'. 'It was here too', Geddie continues, 'on a rainy Sunday, that the author of "Guy Mannering" made his first plunge into love, by offering his umbrella and his escort home to the beautiful young lady, Miss Belsches Stuart, who nearly broke his heart when she married Sir William Forbes, the banker – by no means the only idyll begun under the frowning and grinning effigies of Death and Time in Greyfriars Churchyard' (see Colinton Castle and Colinton House).

Like the other houses in George Square, the three-storeyed No. 25 is rubble-built with large, prominent quoins, and two sturdy Roman Doric columns, below a frieze and cornice, flank the entrance. The square remained a fashionable quarter long after the exodus to the New Town had got under way but was gradually taken over by the University of Edinburgh in the earlier years of the present century.

Gilmerton

A few houses of 18th and early 19th century date have survived in Ravenscroft Street in Gilmerton. Among them are WESTLAND HOUSE and JOFFVILLE, its gable facing the street, both dating from the late 18th century. ANNVILLE, No. 96, with a Roman Doric doorway, is early 19th. Some cottages of the old village also remain, now converted into shops, in Drum Street (See The Drum and Kingston Grange).

At Moredun, near Gilmerton, are the aluminium-covered 'pre-fab' houses built at Craigour in the late 1940s. Quickly assembled and designed as emergency housing with an intended lifespan of ten years, they have nevertheless provided satisfactory and highly valued accommodation down to the present day. Because of structural problems some have recently been pulled down, but those that remain are now owned by those who live in them and who have no desire to move out. Some of these houses, after a life of fity years, are now listed and thus are protected for the future.

Gracemount House

Built about 1800 but incorporating earlier work, Gracemount House was acquired by the city for use as a Youth Centre in 1958 and two schools have now been constructed within its grounds off Lasswade Road. The name of the area, originally Priest's Hill or Priesthill, was changed to Gracemount after the Reformation. The frontage of this much altered and now rather unattractive mansionhouse forms a double bow on either side of the pedimented entrance. Stone carvings can be seen on the north wall and, although these do not appear to be ecclesiastical, it is known that the priest of St. Katherine's lived here when it was called Priesthill.

Grange Court

Approached through two pends on the west side of Causewayside is the secluded Grange Court recalling earlier times when handloom weaving (see Tipperlinn House) flourished here in the otherwise vanished hamlet of Sciennes (see Sciennes Hill House and No. 16 St. Catherine's Place). The Court, dating back to the 1750s, contained fifty-two pantiled weavers' houses, each consisting of either one or two rooms, as well as stables. As the cottage industry of weaving declined, slaughter houses were introduced into the Court with the result that the district deteriorated, and from around

1850 the Causewayside area became overcrowded and law and order were not always maintained among the inhabitants.

Grange Court, however, had the good fortune to be rescued in 1970 (after a demolition order had been placed on all its buildings) when, in spite of the prevailing South Side planning blight, a decision was taken to restore the Court as far as might be possible. The artisan houses on the north side were rehabilitated, including the large projecting stair-tower with an open entrance out of which the lower steps emerge into the courtyard. The stables were replaced by several stone-faced modern houses, and a landscaped plot of small trees and plants was laid out in the centre of the revitalised Court where the old weavers' houses provide a unique insight into one aspect of 18th century domestic architecture and a historic environment in which the housing needs of modern times can be fully realised.

Grange Park

Frederick Thomas Pilkington (1832–98) was a Victorian architect in the Romantic-Gothick mould whose best-known Edinburgh building is the Barclay Church in Bruntsfield. He was the son of an architect and commenced practising on his own account in 1860.

Egremont, the house which he designed for himself in 1864 at No. 38 Dick Place and which is now called Grange Park, is one of several from his drawing-board in this area. Romanesque in derivation, it is a large, elaborately ornate residence of two main storeys with attic and basement, and a central projection is the principal feature of the south, or garden, front which looks out over lawns to the Carlton Cricket Ground. The equally extravagant interior displays many details based on the style prevalent in France during the late 18th century.

Grange Park is no longer, having been sub-divided, in its original condition (see Dean Park House and Kingston Grange).

Greenpark

The old hamlet of Greenend was completely changed when the road to Dalkeith, which formerly passed through the grounds of Kingston Grange (q.v.), was made at the end of the 19th century, at which time a few thatched cottages were still in existence in Greenend.

One of the principal features of the village was the impressive, three-storeyed, stone-built house called Greenpark with its beautiful and well-kept grounds. The main block is recessed between two gabled wings and has a central gabled chimney stack above a prominently projecting portico. The mansion was formerly in the possession of Richard Whytock whose business of tapestry weaving was located in the house. Greenpark latterly became the Scottish Area Headquarters of the National Coal Board.

Greenend House was once part of the largely vanished hamlet of Greenend at Liberton.

The former Mayfield Road Toll-House now rebuilt in Ellen's Glen Loan.

The charming little two-storeyed dwelling which now has the name of GREENEND HOUSE, with astragaled windows, central doorway and one high, far-viewing gable window to the south, is another survivor. Not so fortunate but still standing in the 1890s was the house, nearly opposite the entrance to Greenpark, which had a lintel stone deeply cut with the words 'Robert Bryden, Portioner, 1722', a portioner being, under Scots law, the holder of a small feu originally part of a greater one.

In Ellen's Glen Loan, not far away, beside the bridge across the Burdiehouse Burn, is 'a house reputed to have been rebuilt, stone by stone, from the old Toll House which once stood in Mayfield Road.' It is a clean-cut little building of one storey with long, narrow windows and a central chimney stack between the ridges of a double-piended roof and is in stark contrast to the rest of its still rural environment.

Another altered but sturdily surviving house, at the north end of Gilmerton Road, is the once Georgian LIBERTON EAST MAINS FARM HOUSE, standing below street level and now the Rob Roy Roadhouse.

Hermitage Of Braid

In 1771 Charles Gordon of Cluny purchased the estate of Braid. Before him it had been in the possession of Sir William Dick, Lord Provost of Edinburgh in 1638, who had bought it in 1631 from Sir Robert Fairlie (see Bruntsfield House and Comiston House). It was Gordon of Cluny who built the present mansion in its wooded valley, now a public park, between Greenbank and

Hermitage of Braid, secluded in a wooded valley beside the Braid Burn, once belonged to the Gordons of Cluny.

Blackford in 1785. Situated on the north bank of the Braid Burn, the picturesque, two-storey villa, in a stylistic mixture of medieval and classical design, is all turrets and crenellation at the roofline and all Venetian-windowed Georgian symmetry below.

The estate, administered by trustees, remained with the descendants of the Gordon family but the mansionhouse and its environs became 'the property of the citizens through the munificence of a Morningside resident, Mr John McDougal', of the Leith grain merchants Herdman & McDougal, in 1938. For some years the house was used as a Scout Hostel and is now a Countryside Ranger and Information Centre.

The little building at the entrance to the Hermitage of Braid has an interesting history. Beside the Braid Church near Morningside Station was a toll-house at which every person coming in to the Tollcross area was obliged to pay the dues before being permitted to proceed. When Morningside began to grow as a residential suburb this tax was seen as an injustice as the people who stayed there were Edinburgh citizens as much as those who still lived in the inner city. Agreement was reached that the toll-house should be moved, and in 1861 it was taken down and re-erected at the then boundary at the Jordan Burn where it remained in service until the abolition of road tolls in Scotland in 1883.

At that time Sir John Skelton (1831–97), the historian and essayist who wrote for *Blackwood's Magazine* under the name of *Shirley*, was living in Hermitage of Braid where he entertained such literary celebrities as Thackeray, Robert Browning and D.G. Rossetti. In 1888 Skelton took over the redundant toll-house and had it rebuilt 'stone by stone, as the entrance lodge to his residence'. The figures 259, its old number in Morningside Road, remained on a lintel at the back of the house, although the door itself was built up. It was at this door that the tolls had been paid, a wheel in a bay window operating the toll-gate.

Hope House or Gairnshall

In the closing years of the 17th century a brewer called Alexander Biggar, heritor, according to Lord Fountainhall's report, of 'the houses called Gairnshall, beyond the Windmill, and built in that myre commonly called the Goose Dub', made legal declaration of his desire to relinquish responsibility for 'watching and warding', a duty he had become obliged to undertake in terms of his feu charter from John Gairns. Gairns himself had acquired the land from the Town Council in 1681, and a row of brewers' houses was then built beside the South or Burgh Loch in the basin of which The Meadows was afterwards laid out after several attempts had been made to solve the intractable drainage problems. It was not until 1863 that the land took on its present appearance as a public park.

The loch was the main source of Edinburgh's water supply until 1596 when it was taken over by the Fellowship and Society of Brewers who used a windmill, which gave its name to Windmill Street nearby, to pump up the water for their Brewery to which it was then conveyed in pipes. By the time the Society was dissolved in 1619 the loch had suffered considerable diminution. Eventually reduced to a morass of marsh and mud, it was Sir Thomas Hope of Rankeillor who was finally successful in draining the ground in the first half of the 18th century.

Standing within the tiny Hope Park Square, its curving Dutch gable with terminating scrolls now unsympathetically joined to its younger neighbours on either side, is Gairnshall, now known as Hope House, built c. 1735 by Sir Thomas Hope of Rankeillor who died here in 1771. It was restored and converted into three flats in 1978.

The building with a projecting stair-tower beside Buccleuch and Greyfriars Free Church in West Crosscauseway, and which was in recent years converted into flats, stands at Quarry Close within a small grass-grown court. (This name is derived from quarry holes here which were once worked in connection with the Goose (or Guse) Dub.) This building is not nearly as old as it appears to be. Constructed in the second half of the 19th century. It was 'a deliberate essay in traditional style' as Stuart Harris, the former Edinburgh City Architect whose invaluable book *The Place Names of Edinburgh* was published in 1996 shortly before his death, has pointed out.

The Inch

'The quaint old Inch House', as Grant describes it, was built in 1617, although little of that date remains today, 'upon land which, in the preceding century, belonged to the monks of Holyrood.' It was erected by a Keeper of the Great Seal of Scotland, James Winram, whose son was raised to the bench in 1649 with the title of Lord Liberton. In accordance with its name, The Inch was originally an island site within a marsh or sheet of water, access being obtained by means of a drawbridge across a moat. It was built as a fortalice, says John Geddie, in a period 'when the possessors of The Inch had to protect themselves against ill neighbours as well as enemies of the realm'.

After the Winrams, 'a strongly Covenanting stock', came, in the year of the Restoration of Charles II, the Gilmours (later Little-Gilmours) of Craigmillar (see Craigmillar Castle, Liberton Tower and Liberton House), who enlarged the house. Finally, as late as 1892, the architects MacGibbon and Ross (see Hillwood House and Braehead) carried out extensive work on the old structure which is today a large and complex building, incorporating fabric from a number of periods, of crowstepped gables, Georgian wings and Victorian bay and oriel windows.

The Inch has been used as a primary school and is now a community centre. The surrounding policies, denuded of their ancient timber, have succumbed to council-house proliferation while the ancient pile, its long memory going back to the days of James VI, broods doggedly upon its changed environment within the noisy limits of a public park.

Kingston Grange

Kingston Grange, off Kingston Avenue at Gilmerton (q.v.), was built by Robert Adam in 1788 and was originally known as Sunnyside. It changed its name with its ownership, says John Geddie, being renamed, when acquired by Colonel Hay of Duns Castle, in memory of his ancestor, Viscount Kingston. This bow-fronted Georgian house was altered in the mid-19th century by

Kingston House, originally Craigend Park, was built by the 19th century architect F.T. Pilkington for an Edinburgh tailor.

Burn & Bryce and is now the Club House of Liberton Golf Course (see Greenpark).

On the corner of Kingston Avenue and Gilmerton Road, and within its own secluded, eight-acre grounds, stands Craigend Park, an extravagantly ornate Victorian mansion built in 1869 by the architect F.T. Pilkington (see Grange Park and Dean Park House) for William Christie, an Edinburgh tailor. This house of many gables, a curved corner entrance and windows derived from several building styles is crowned by a round, balustraded tower to which is attached a high, slender turret with a conical roof. A long tree-lined drive winds from the entrance gates towards the house which, from

1938 until 1984, was a nature cure centre called the Kingston Clinic.
It is now known as KINGSTON HOUSE.

Liberton Bank House

Beside the Braid Burn at the north end of Gilmerton Road near
Nether Liberton, and part of a historic group of buildings (see
Nether Liberton House), is the 18th century, single-storey Liberton
Bank House. The writer Conan Doyle spent part of his boyhood in
the house which was owned by his father. It has been boarded up
for some years.

Nearby is LIBERTON GREEN HOUSE, also built in the 18th
century but having many later alterations.

Liberton House

The old mansion of North or Upper Liberton now known as
Liberton House is, says John Geddie, 'in many ways a charac-
teristic example of the domestic architecture and arrangements of
the early 17th century.' A transitional building, it exhibits features of
both the towerhouse and manorhouse eras. Constructed (the exact
date is uncertain) probably on the site of a previous building, the
L-plan mansionhouse has a main block of three storeys with small and
irregularly spaced windows, a four-floor wing and a stair tower in the
re-entrant angle with gunloops through which the entrance could be
defended. There are additions, alterations and restorations of many
different dates, all of which have made this ancient house, entered
from Liberton Drive, a building of considerable complexity.

It belonged originally to the merchant William Little (see Liberton Tower and The Inch) who acquired the estate in 1587 and
whose son, Clement, founded the Library of Edinburgh University.
Continuing in the possession of that family, the last representative
to occupy the house was General Sir Gordon Gilmour, Bart., a
descendant of the Littles. Since then it has been in residential use
but plans drawn up in 1982 for its incorporation into a country
club did not materialise. The Braid Burn flows through the

The L-plan Liberton House in Liberton Drive before the fire which preceded its restoration.

grounds and Liberton House can lay claim to those two gratifying concomitants of ancient dwellings, a ghost and a doocot. The former is but rarely seen, though the latter, being exceptional in size, stands substantially within the gates.

The roof and upper storey were badly damaged by fire in 1991 but the house has now been fully restored by the architect Nicholas Groves-Raines.

Also in Liberton is the Georgian farmhouse of BURDIEHOUSE MAINS, and nearby, at the top of Lasswade Road, is the two-storeyed former KIRK FARMHOUSE, white-walled with the exception of the large gable which abuts the street. It was built in the 18th century, and a lower courtyard range lies on its southern side.

Liberton Tower

The 15th century Liberton Tower still dourly keeps its distance, well over four hundred feet above sea level, on a spur of the Braid Hills at Upper, or Over, Liberton. It has two entrances; one at ground level gives access to the basement, while the other on the first floor was reached by means of an outside timber forestair and a landing. The massive thick-walled structure has four storeys, two with vaulted ceilings, and three spiral stairs. A gallery of stone or wooden beams around the wallhead would have provided a look-out point and embrasures for defence, and, if the house was well provisioned, the occupants would have had a good chance of fighting off attack. An early owner was William Little, Lord Provost of Edinburgh from 1586–91 (see Liberton House and The Inch).

Built as a farmhouse about 1830, Liberton Tower Mains is now a private residence.

At one time, according to some accounts, a robber laird held the old Tower of Liberton and kept his household well supplied with victuals by making periodic raids on produce carts on their peaceful way to the Old Town of Edinburgh.

Liberton Tower has recently been tastefully restored and is now fit for residential use.

The former farmhouse of LIBERTON TOWER MAINS lies among grass and trees off the west side of Liberton Brae. Built about 1830, this interesting and attractive Georgian house consists of a central block of two storeys with lower wings at each side. The chimneys are confined to either end of the main gables, and pleasing features high on the gable walls are the small, round-headed windows containing Georgian glazing. This secluded building is now a private house but retains its original name of Liberton Tower Mains.

Mansewood

The house now known as Mansewood is a plain, two-storeyed and bay-windowed villa, half hidden by a hedge and trees, at No. 52 Morningside Park, but its existence constitutes a direct link with the old Morningside House which once stood southwards of the site of the present Morningside Public Library and which eventually became No. 200 Morningside Road.

In the 18th century Morningside House belonged to the Judge, Lord Gardenstone, and in 1795 it was sold by his nephew to David Deuchar (1742–1808), etcher and seal engraver to the Prince Regent (later George IV). He also 'discovered' the future Sir Henry Raeburn (1756–1823), who was then apprenticed to a jeweller in the Parliament Close, and introduced him to the Edinburgh painter David Martin whose pupil Raeburn then became. Deuchar died at Morningside House in 1808 and the property descended to other members of his family, coming finally into the possession of his grandson, David Deuchar, F.R.S.E., the Manager of the Caledonian Insurance Company in Edinburgh, who built the house in what later became Morningside Park in 1874. He then removed from Morningside House to his new villa, giving it the name of Harlaw. (Morningside House was demolished about twenty years later.) Continuing to live at Harlaw until 1881, he then sold it, as a manse, to Morningside Parish Church, and it was when this use came to an end that the name was changed, appropriately, to Mansewood.

It is interesting to note that Morningside Place was formerly known as Deuchar Street, and that, by a strange coincidence, the pictorial headings of the first policies issued by the Caledonian Insurance Company were designed by Raeburn.

A few restored and occupied cottages from the heart of old Morningside are out of sight behind Morningside Road and are approached by a short lane beside *The Merlin* at No. 168 Morningside Road. The three old cottages in Springvalley Terrace (formerly Rosewood Place) are ROSEWOOD COTTAGE, PENTIRE COTTAGE and VIEWHILL COTTAGE, now known as Viewhill House, which is a substantial detached family house built in 1825.

HOPEFIELD COTTAGE, No. 17 Greenhill Gardens, was built for Dr John Kirk of the Evangelical Union in 1851. His son John, minister of Gorgie Evangelical Church, lived and, in 1923, died in Hopefield Cottage where David Livingstone had been a visitor, and it was his wife, in order to raise funds for his church, who sold handwritten copies of recipes for one penny, the demand for which was so great that they were published and became famous under the title *Tried Favourites* which no housewife worth her salt for many years to come was ever without. A member of this family was still living here in the 1930s. Sir John Steell, who designed so many of Edinburgh's commemorative monuments, lived opposite at No. 24 Greenhill Gardens.

Morton House

Standing serenely at the end of Winton Loan at Fairmilehead, Morton House was built in 1702 as a plain, gable-ended dwellinghouse with a large chimney gable in the centre of the east, or main, front. In 1805, however, the house was reorientated in the opposite direction when an addition with an elegant Georgian façade was built behind it facing the two ogival-roofed pavilions at the gate, both buildings being clearly differentiable when viewed from the side. A two-storeyed belvedere, built on grassland beyond

Morton House at Fairmilehead with the 1805 frontage beyond one of the two ogival-roofed pavilions at the gate.

the garden, together with the immaculate garden itself, provide the house with an environment that could hardly be improved upon.

In the late 18th century the house was purchased by the Trotters of Mortonhall (see Mortonhall House, Swanston Cottage and Colinton House) for use as a dowerhouse, and it was here that John Hill Burton died in 1881, about a hundred years later, after his reluctant move from Old Craig House (q.v.) some years before.

Mortonhall House

The Trotter family, planters of the 'T' Wood above Swanston, have had a long association with Edinburgh (see Morton House,

Swanston Cottage and Colinton House). Known as the Trotters of Mortonhall, their house of that name was built in 1769 by the architect John Baxter, Jnr. This large, secluded Georgian building of three storeys and basement has a wide pediment at roof level on both front and rear elevations and a pedimented portico (added in the 19th century) flanked by twin Doric columns.

The mansion, which was used as a nursing home for some years while still in the possession of the Trotter family, and is surrounded by gardens and extensive parkland, is entered from Frogston Road East and has been converted into flats.

Morton house showing the 1805 addition behind the original house built in 1702.

Now converted into flats, the mansionhouse of Mortonhall was built by the Trotters of Mortonhall in 1769.

Nether Liberton House

The tall chimneys and white-harled walls of Nether Liberton House form an attractive composition near an interesting and very ancient group of buildings, mostly with a milling connection, at the north end of Gilmerton Road (see Liberton Bank House). The house was once a coaching inn and till 1850 had a licence to retail liquor. In more recent times it was the home of the late John P. Mackintosh, M.P.

Nether Liberton House was built in the 18th century but was enlarged by the addition of a second storey and remodelled about 1840.

At the north end of Gilmerton Road the 18th century Nether Liberton House was once a coaching inn.

Old Craig House

Old Craig House, on Easter Craiglockhart Hill, was set on fire by the Earl of Hertford during his hostile advance into Scotland in 1544, the house, or what remained of it, then being acquired by Laurence Symsoune by whom it was rebuilt in 1565. This date and his initials, together with those of his wife Catherine Pringle, can still be seen above the entrance to the stair-tower. Vaulted rooms on the ground floor are all that is left of the original house and date back to 1528. An addition, consisting of a long north wing, was built in 1746 by Sir John Elphinstone who placed the Elphinstone arms in a carved stone panel above the door.

In the 19th century Old Craig House became the home of John Hill Burton, LL.D. (1809–81), Historiographer Royal in Scotland, whose famous library (the floors are said to have been shored up to support its weight) extended over many rooms. It is recorded that he could enter any of them in the dark and go straight to the book he required without hesitation. Hill Burton lived in this isolated spot from 1861 to 1878 and left regretfully, and only for another house of many summers (see Morton House), when its sixty-one-acre environs were acquired for the construction of the large Victorian Craighouse Asylum of which Old Craig House now became a part.

When the Thomas Clouston Clinic, as it was later called, was closed, the whole site was purchased, in 1994, by Napier University as its Craighouse Campus. Extensive restoration work was undertaken by the University and one of the most interesting discoveries in Old Craig House, in a room next to the dining-room, was the leather wall covering which, as it had been hidden from sight for many years, still retains its brightly coloured red and gold decoration of flowers and birds in remarkable preservation. Alterations to the house carried out by the Asylum are recorded by the date, 1878, placed on the fireplace of the dining-room on the first floor of the north wing.

Old Craig House, on Easter Craiglockhart Hill, dates back to the 16th century and is now incorporated in the Craighouse Campus of Napier University.

Pear Tree or West Nicolson House

Built c. 1747 for the merchant William Reid, West Nicolson House, or Pear Tree House as it is more usually called from the jargonelle pear tree, said to have been planted about the middle of the 19th century, which grows across the west-facing frontage, stands on the corner of Chapel Street and West Nicolson Street behind walls which also encompass an open yard in front of the building. A principal feature of the house is the high central gable containing two windows below a triangular pediment, which emphasises the texture of the rubble walls.

An early occupant was the judge Lord Kilkerran who died in 1759. The house then passed to Sir Adam Fergusson, Member of Parlia-

West Nicolson house, better known as Pear Tree House, seen through the open entrance in West Nicolson Street.

ment for Edinburgh in the 1780s, and it was during his period of ownership that many legal celebrities, including James Boswell, were frequent guests. The Rev. Dr Thomas Blacklock, the blind poet and patron of Robert Burns, lived on the two upper floors and had the distinction of entertaining Dr Johnson here in 1773 (see Sciennes Hill House).

Pear Tree House was altered and extended eastwards to provide office accommodation after its purchase in 1823 by the brewer Andrew Usher who placed the monogram of the House of Usher on the base of the round glass cupola. It was a bequest from a member of this family which financed the building, in 1911, of the Usher Hall in Lothian Road and it is claimed that the Usher Hall dome bears a strong resemblance to the cupola in Pear Tree House. Inside are the curving panelled 'hanging' staircase between the upper floors and a panelled bedroom containing a bed recess.

The house has for a long time been in commercial ownership, the previous occupants being the whisky merchants J. & G. Stewart Ltd. who acquired the property in 1919 and who moved to Leith in 1970. It remained unoccupied for six years and was considered by the Town Council, but rejected as unsuitable, as a possible location for the City Art Centre. The whole building is now used as *The Peartree* and *The Blind Poet* public houses, the latter in commemoration of Dr Blacklock and here, on part of the stairs, wall panels display extracts from a few of his poems.

Prestonfield House

The first recorded reference to the lands of Prestonfield or Priestfield, when they were granted to the monks of Harehope in Northumberland, is in a Royal Charter of 1153, although they reverted to the Crown in 1355 when David II of Scotland was released from captivity in England, the monks, who had given their support to Edward III, being punished by a withdrawal of their grant.

The estate, after several ownerships, passed to the Hamiltons, 'one of whom, Thomas', says Grant, 'fell at Flodden in 1513'. Sir Alexander Hamilton, brother of the first Earl of Haddington, 'departed this lyffe at Priestfield, neire Edinburghe' in 1649, and the

Prestonfield house, in Priestfield Road, is now an hotel but was once the home of Sir Alexander Dick of Prestonfield who entertained Dr Johnson here during his visit to Scotland.

lands were purchased in 1677 by James Dick, a wealthy merchant and Lord Provost of the city, when he was created a baronet of Nova Scotia. This family later, through marriage, assumed the name of Dick-Cunyngham, and have continued in uninterrupted possession down to the present time.

Sir James's grandson, Sir Alexander Dick of Prestonfield, became a noted physician, accompanied the young Scottish portrait painter Allan Ramsay (see Ramsay Lodge) on the obligatory Grand Tour of Europe in 1736 and entertained Prince Charles Edward Stuart at Prestonfield House in 1745. Later visitors were James Boswell, who at one time contemplated writing a biography of Sir Alexander Dick, and Dr Johnson. Dick pioneered the cultivation of rhubarb, 'and Dr Johnson was among those to whom he sent supplies of this revolutionary plant, which he nurtured on his Prestonfield estate.'

The first house, called Priestfield, was situated on the same site as its successor on the south side of the Queen's Park and was burned down in 1681 by rioting students. Sir Alexander having friends in high places, his new residence was paid for by the Scottish Treasury. The architect was Sir William Bruce, who designed the extension of Holyrood Palace (q.v.), who brought with him the craftsmen he had employed to carry out the work, commissioned by Charles II, at the royal residence. Completed in 1687, the present Prestonfield House has a splendid white-harled frontage of two floors and basement, rising to three storeys at each side of the west-facing main facade where the two windows in each of the upper floors are crowned by curvilinear 'Dutch' gables supporting chimney stacks. Balustrading links the lower portions of the gables, and at ground level an imposing Roman Doric-columned *porte cochère*, added in 1818, projects beyond the entrance.

The oval ballroom and dining-room were built about 1815 and are still hung with Dick family portraits dating from the late 17th century. In the tapestry room is the famous plaster ceiling, with vigorous pendant cupids and heraldic beasts, which is comparable to similar work at Holyrood, and the Spanish leather hangings in a former bedroom were bought for Sir James Dick in Cordova in 1676. Not far from the mansionhouse are the circular stables built in 1816.

In beautiful grounds and entered from Priestfield Road, this fine old house has been an hotel for many years.

St. Bennet's

The house called St. Bennet's, No. 42 Greenhill Gardens, was built in the mid-19th century. A crowstepped, baronial pile with gables and a little corbelled tower, it stands behind a wall with an early 20th century chapel in front. A sundial from the mansion of Grange House, which was demolished in 1936, was re-erected in the front garden at St. Bennet's. All that remains of Grange House are the re-sited 18th century Lauder Wyverns on their ornamental columns in Grange Loan.

St. Bennet's is the residence of the Roman Catholic Archbishop of St. Andrews and Edinburgh, one of its recent occupants being Cardinal Gordon Gray (1910–93).

St. Bennet's, in Greenhill Gardens, is the residence of the Bishop of St. Andrews and Edinburgh. The chapel in front was built in the early 20th century.

No. 16 St. Catherine's Place

The historic interest at No. 16 St. Catherine's Place centres not on the house itself but on the small front garden where a plaque attached to a little pile of stones records that

> This house occupies the site of the last fragment of The Convent of St. Catherine of Sienna, erected 1517, demolished 1871.

The convent was founded on the Burgh Muir by Lady Jane Hepburn, widow of the third Earl of Seton, and two other noble-women whose husbands had been slain in 1513 on Flodden field. In Volume I of *Historic South Edinburgh* Charles J. Smith writes: 'The site of the convent was the south-east end of Sciennes Road and its walls encompassed both sides of present-day St. Catherine's Place.'

The surrounding district of Sciennes takes its name from Scienne which, says Charles J. Smith, is 'the French version of Sienna'.

St. Katherine's

Off Howdenhall Road opposite Mortonhall Crematorium is the house called St. Katherine's. Built in the year 1806, its grounds now surrounded by the suburban streets of Gracemount and Liberton, it was enlarged and altered several times during the following century and stands beside the old Balm Well of St. Katherine which can still be seen a few hundred yards in front of the house. The well, according to legend, sprang up when St. Katherine – her true

St. Katherine's, beside the Balm Well, and photographed in 1986, was built in 1806.

identity is unknown – who had brought holy oil from the tomb of St. Katherine of Alexandria at Mount Sinai, happened to spill a few drops at that spot while on her way to deliver it to St. Margaret, the queen of Malcolm Canmore, at whose request she had made the journey. James VI, during his only visit to Scotland, in 1617, after becoming King of England, visited the well and had it enclosed in richly ornamented stonework, including a door and steps to make access less difficult for the infirm who sought healing in its waters which, when analysed many years afterwards, were found to contain petroleum. The structure was severely damaged by Cromwell's troops in 1650 but some repairs were made after the Restoration.

The house of St. Katherine's (or St. Catherine's) has had many occupants, the most noteworthy being the Lord Advocate Sir William Rae who conducted the trial of Burke, the associate of Hare, in one of the most famous criminal proceedings in the legal history of Edinburgh. Sir Walter Scott dined at the house in 1825, as he recorded in his Journal.

A children's home, now run by The City of Edinburgh Council, was built in the grounds of St. Katherine's and the house itself suffered vandalism. However, the building has recently been fully restored and is now a lounge bar and restaurant.

An interesting footnote to the story of this house and its environs is the fact that it constituted a staging post for the mail coaches travelling between Edinburgh and London, and an old milestone stood near the house until it was accidentally destroyed some years ago.

Sciennes Hill House

The district of Sciennes beside The Meadows recalls the 16th century Convent of St. Catherine of Sienna (see No. 16 St. Catherine's Place). In Sciennes House Place (formerly Braid Place) stands Sciennes Hill House (No. 7), now incorporated in tenemental property and sadly altered and deteriorated from its original condition although restoration work was carried out in 1989. Built in 1741, this was the home of Dr Adam Fergusson, Professor of Moral Philosophy at Edinburgh University, whose son, Sir Adam (see Pear Tree House), was a lifelong friend of Sir Walter Scott, and it was here that the brief but famous meeting of Scott and Robert Burns took place in the winter of 1786–7.

Scott himself has described in his Journal the occasion when, as 'a lad of fifteen', he saw Burns 'one day at the venerable Professor Fergusson's where there were several gentlemen of literary reputation.' He remembered the poet's interest in a print showing a scene on 'Minden's plain' after the battle when, in 1759, the French were defeated by an allied army which included British soldiers, and his inability to recall the author of the affecting lines of verse that were reproduced beneath it. 'It chanced', wrote Scott, 'that nobody but myself remembered that they occur in a half-forgotten poem of Langhorne's called by the unpromising title of *The Justice of the Peace*. I whispered my information to a friend present, who mentioned it to Burns, who rewarded me with a look and a word, which, though of mere civility, I then received, and still recollect, with very great pleasure.' Burns was then aged twenty-eight.

This once free-standing mansion has been converted into flats and, like several other Edinburgh houses, turned back to front, the former main elevation now overlooking an enclosed back-green into which it was necessary to penetrate in order to read the tablet high on the wall, where it was originally placed, recording the meeting between Burns and Scott. This tablet has now been resited on the street frontage in Sciennes House Place although access is available between 2 and 5 p.m. to view the restored original main facade. The original entrance, once reached by a flight of steps and now blocked up, can still be seen at first-floor level. This street of working men's dwellinghouses was built c. 1870 (see George Square, Atholl Crescent and North Castle Street).

Swanston Cottage

Clinging to the northern foothills of the Pentlands, the little 18th century, thatch-roofed hill village of Swanston (which is now a conservation area) has been kept since 1962 in a state of rural preservation, its individual cottages inhabited, beside the flowing burn and with only the green upland grass for street and pavement.

A short distance away and sheltered among trees stands Swanston Cottage, or Swanston House, built in 1761 by Edinburgh Town

A restored thatched cottage beside the green at Swanston.

Council (after they had got the better of Trotter of Mortonhall (see Morton House and Mortonhall House), to whom the ground belonged, who resisted the proposal with might and vehemence) as part of their scheme to augment the city's water supply. The house was not, of course, essential to the plan, but when pipes had been laid to carry the spring water to the town it occurred to these worthy magistrates that, as Stevenson expressed it in his *Picturesque Notes*, 'the place was suitable for junketing'. The original building was in all respects a typical country cottage, but it eventually blossomed into a fairly spacious, two-storey and bow-fronted house, though some of the additions were made in the 19th century. 'They brought crockets and gargoyles from old St. Giles, which they were then restoring', wrote R.L.S., 'and disposed them on the gables and over the door and about the garden.' 'And at night', he continued, 'from high upon the hills a shepherd saw lighted windows through the foliage and heard the voice of city dignitaries raised in song.'

The Stevenson connection with the house began in 1867, when the poet's father, Thomas Stevenson, rented it as a holiday cottage, and lasted approximately fifteen years. Robert Louis himself dearly loved this Pentland retreat and from it he roamed the hills, often in the company of John Todd, 'the roaring shepherd', and included Swanston in his novel *St. Ives*, a tale of the Napoleonic Wars written in 1894, at the end of his life, in Samoan exile (see Baxter's Place, Pilrig House, Howard Place, Heriot Row and Colinton Manse).

Between 1908 and 1924 a friend and contemporary of Stevenson, Lord Guthrie, lived in Swanston Cottage where he assembled a

Swanston Cottage in the Pentland Hills was rented by the father of Robert Louis Stevenson as a summer residence in 1867.

collection of R.L.S. memorabilia. Further alterations to the house were carried out for him by Sir Robert Lorimer. This historic house was until the early 1980s owned and leased by the city authorities. They have, however, seen fit to sell it and it is now in private ownership.

Nearby is the large, 17th century, crowstep-gabled SWANSTON OLD FARMHOUSE, built round three sides of a square, which has now been restored and sub-divided for residential occupation.

Sylvan Hut

In the second half of the 18th century the building of small, 'weekend' residences, referred to as 'huts', in the countryside a short distance out of town became popular among those city inhabitants who occupied large and imposing houses. Quite often they were fairly substantial buildings, as was certainly the case with Sylvan Hut (also known as William's Hut) which is a two-storey Georgian house off Sylvan Place near the junction of Sciennes and Warrender Park Roads, and is approached by a narrow lane. Built in the 1760s (and now No. 13 Sylvan Place) in the grounds of the demolished Leven Lodge (the country villa of the Earls of Leven (see Gayfield House)) by an advocate called Joseph Williamson, Sylvan Hut stands behind a little garden and has astragaled windows and a segmental pediment above the door.

Tipperlinn House

The old weavers' hamlet of Tipperlinn at Morningside has been swept away, 'in 1853 the remaining portions of the quaint little village', says William Mair, being incorporated into the grounds of what was then called the Royal Mental Hospital. Tipperlinn House, behind its gate-piers by the roadside leading to the Hospital, was built on part of the site of the old village as a residence for the Physician Superintendent (though no longer used as such) and is an undistinguished building enhanced by the old trees and lawns that lie behind it.

When the weaving industry was at its height, linen damask was woven at Tipperlinn where almost every cottage had its hand loom until technical advances put an end to cottage industries (see Grange Court).

Westgate House

No. 1 Churchhill is the house formerly called Churchhill and now known as Westgate House. It was built in 1842 for Dr Thomas Chalmers (1780–1847), Professor of Divinity at Edinburgh University. He had lived previously at No. 7 INVERLEITH

Westgate House at Churchhill, with plaque on wall at left, was built by Dr Chalmers in the year before the Disruption.

ROW. After the Disruption in the following year, when Dr Chalmers became the first Moderator of the Free Church of Scotland, he preached in the house for several weeks 'planted midway up the staircase to a disjointed congregation scattered over the different rooms' (*Memoirs of Dr Chalmers* by William Hanna). Its members later formed the new congregation of the Free Church (now the Baptist Church in Morningside Road) built later in 1843 and of which Dr Chalmers became minister.

A bronze tablet on the south-facing frontage of his house, a large Georgian-style villa with astragaled windows and a central projection containing the doorway and surmounted at roof level by a triangular pediment, records that 'In this house Thomas Chalmers died, 31st May 1847.'

A statue of Dr Chalmers by Sir John Steell was erected in 1876 at the intersection of George Street and Castle Street.

Whitehouse

There are two houses in Whitehouse Loan called the Whitehouse. The later of these, No. 17, white-walled and with a pedimented frontage, was built c. 1840. (SYDNEY LODGE at No. 21 is of similar date.)

The older and more interesting mansion of Whitehouse was built in 1670 and it is this house which has given its name to Whitehouse Loan. In 1835 it was incorporated by the architect James Gillespie Graham into the then new buildings of St. Margaret's Convent when an ogee-roofed entrance tower was added at the north end. Externally only a very small section of the house is visible, but this cannot be seen from the street. The convent later became St. Margaret's School and, later still, Gillis College.

Bishop Gillis, one of the founders of the convent, lived latterly in GREENHILL COTTAGE, where he died in 1864 and was buried in the convent chapel, in Greenhill Terrace, the house being used latterly in conjunction with Bruntsfield Hospital which was closed in 1988 and bought by Napier Polytechnic (now Napier University) in 1991.

There is also a Whitehouse at Barnton (q.v.) and another, which was once the schoolhouse, in the village of Swanston.

Woodburn House

This plain Georgian house in Canaan Lane, with two dormer windows above the main frontage where a prominent portico with Roman Doric columns projects beyond the entrance doorway, was built at a cost of £300 in 1812. The earliest occupant was George Ross, an advocate. In 1861 D.R. McGregor of the Merchant Shipping Co. of Leith lived in the house which was later a Sanatorium, then a Nurses' Home of the Edinburgh Royal Infirmary and in recent years a Health Education Centre.

D. West Edinburgh

Baberton House

Built by Sir James Murray, Master of Works to James VI, in 1622, Baberton (anciently, says John Geddie, Kilbaberton) House stands within nine acres of ground between Juniper Green and Wester Hailes. It may have been used by King James as a hunting lodge and was with certainty occupied by Charles X of France (see Holyrood Palace) when, in exile after his abdication in 1830, he sought, for the second time, refuge and a debtor's sanctuary at Holyrood. The dining-room, panelled in Memel pine, was his salon when staying at Baberton, and other original features of the house include vaulted ground-floor rooms and spiral stairs. An addition was made to the old building in 1765 when a three-storey, semi-octagonal wing was built to fill in the double L-plan of the original three-storey house on the southern side. The walled garden contains a tennis court and a pavilion.

Baberton House went out of private ownership in 1977 and is now used as office accommodation by Cruden Investments Ltd.

Beechmount

Beechmount, at the top of a steeply rising path, was built in 1900 and stands on the south side of Corstorphine Hill. Together with eight acres of ground, it was left to the Royal Infirmary of Edinburgh in 1926 by a former treasurer of the Bank of Scotland, Sir George Anderson, and his wife. By specific request it was to be used as a residential home for officers disabled in the First World War and also for their families, but its facilities were later made available to the general public.

The house is a heavy and pretentious building surrounded by

projecting bay windows. At one corner is a tower which terminates in an open, arcaded dome.

Beechwood

B uilt in 1780 for a Scott of Harden, this somewhat plain mansion-house near the Edinburgh Zoo consists of a central two-storeyed block with basement and attic floors, and two lower wings on either side which were added at a later date, the house being enlarged about 1799 for Robert Dundas by the New Town architect, William Sibbald.

This was the residence of Sir Robert Dundas of Perthshire (of the same line as the Dundases of Arniston) who inherited it and the surrounding estate on the death of his uncle, General Sir David Dundas, and died in 1835.

Beechwood is now in use by the Murrayfield Hospital which opened in 1984.

Belmont

T he original house on this Murrayfield site was known as Bruce-hill, the ground having been purchased by Charles Bruce, an Edinburgh glazier, in the third decade of the 18th century, from John Dickie (see Corstorphine Hill House), a merchant in the city, who had acquired land on the southern side of Corstorphine Hill about ten years earlier. The twenty-two-acre estate was laid out with orchards and a bowling green. Brucehill and its grounds were then bought by a lawyer, David Campbell, in 1762 and it was he who gave it the name of Belmont by which it has since been known. Twelve years afterwards the failure of the Ayr Bank brought about his financial ruin and he emigrated to New York.

In 1827 the estate was acquired by Joshua Mackenzie, the law lord son of Henry Mackenzie, author of *The Man of Feeling* (see Henry Mackenzie's Cottage), when the old house was demolished and W.H. Playfair approached to design a new one which was built the following year. Surrounded by its beautiful garden, Belmont is an

Belmont, built in 1828, is a grand Italian villa at Murrayfield.

Italian-style villa with deeply projecting eaves borrowed from a southern country much more in need of protection from the sun than windswept Edinburgh.

In 1853 the Hope family took over the property and it remained in their ownership for three generations. Thereafter, in 1930, part of the ground was utilised to widen Ellersly Road, and modern housing was built on part of the estate. This work was carried out by the builder James, later Sir James, Miller, who was later Lord Provost of Edinburgh and Lord Mayor of London, Belmont becoming his family home.

Nearby are the noteworthy houses of Easter Belmont, including EASTER BELMONT HOUSE and BELMONT LODGE. Another Georgian house in Ellersly Road is HARMONY LODGE with a bold central projection between two irregular wings, one of which is single-storeyed and the other two-storeyed with a pedimented window on the upper floor of the main frontage. It has a small lodge cottage and the grounds extend to approximately two acres.

INNERWICK HOUSE, also in Ellersly Road, with two storeys and an attractive Georgian doorway, was built c. 1700 and has Victorian additions. In the interior is a D-ended music room on the ground floor. The coach-house in the grounds has a separate entrance in Murrayfield Road.

KINELLAN, No. 33 Murrayfield Road, was built in 1846 and enlarged in 1913 by Sir Robert Lorimer. In its grounds, just over two acres in extent, a number of modern houses have been erected in recent years. The house itself has been converted into flats.

Bonaly Tower

This house, of somewhat unusual appearance, was largely the creation of Henry Cockburn (1779–1854), who wrote of its building, 'to a great extent with my own hands', in his *Memorials*. He did, however, have the assistance of W.H. Playfair after purchasing, in 1811, an old farmhouse below the Pentland Hills at Colinton around which to design a country seat and a place of retirement which never ceased to give pleasure both to him and his literary associates. Completed as late as 1836, with alterations by David Bryce just thirty years later, the tall, slender tower in the angle of the house gives the impression, to 20th century eyes, of a stately rocket newly launched and lifting off between the trees.

Like Scott at Abbotsford, Lord Cockburn assembled at Bonaly a collection of carved stones from old, dismantled buildings – garden urns, vases and statuary – including the figure of Shakespeare from the original Theatre Royal at the east end of Princes Street. In 1888 a library wing was added to the house by the architect Sydney Mitchell, but sub-division into flats has taken place in more recent times.

Henry Cockburn (see Charlotte Square) was appointed a judge of the Court of Session in 1834 with the title of Lord Cockburn. He wrote on political and legal matters and was the biographer of his friend and fellow judge, Lord Jeffrey (see Craigcrook Castle). Thomas Carlyle called him 'small, solid and genuine . . . A gentleman, I should say, and perfectly in the Scotch type, perhaps the very last of the peculiar species.' He died in 1854 at Bonaly where, in his own words, he had 'destroyed a village and erected a tower, and reached the dignity of a twenty-acred laird.'

Bonaly Tower at Colinton was the creation of Lord Cockburn and W.H. Playfair.

The neo-Gothick BONALY FARMHOUSE, a distance of half a mile from Lord Cockburn's 'Pentland Eden', was a late Victorian reconstruction of a much less grandiose building of the 1860s. The house has fifteen rooms, and a curved staircase rises from the entrance hall. There is a long, low extension to the east. This badly deteriorated structure has been rescued, carefully restored and is again inhabited and, although much of its surrounding land has been disposed of, a huge lawn is overlooked by the north-facing frontage with its gable, turret and bay window.

Braehead

Every student of Scottish history knows the tale, apocryphal or otherwise, of the Guidman of Ballengeich – of how King James V going, disguised, about his realm, fell foul of marauding gypsies near the Cramond Brig. It was Jock Howison, a local miller, who rescued him and who was given the lands of Braehead as his reward.

Jock Howison's cottage was by the River Almond below Cramond Brig and some old building stones, the remains of what appears to have been a little two-roomed dwelling embedded in the grass, are traditionally claimed to be the remains of JOCK HOWISON'S COTTAGE, though this is improbable. A fanciful depiction of James's rescue, now located at the former Braehead Mains on the west side of Queensferry Road, was created by the sculptor, Robert Forrest, about 1836.

The mansion of Braehead lies away from the river to the west of Whitehouse Road at Barnton. It was built at the beginning of the 18th century but has a late Victorian extension with a prominent crowstepped gable facing the gate-piers which once stood at the end of a long drive entered from Braehead Road. Now, however, since the grounds were sold to a developer, suburban pathways have been beaten to its gates and a modern residential enclave laid out within sight of the house.

In Whitehouse Road, on the Cramond side of Braehead, is THE WHITEHOUSE, white-harled and with a large re-entrant-angle stair turret, an early 17th century residence built by the Primrose family but extended in the 18th century and altered by MacGibbon and Ross at the end of the 19th.

The Bush

On the south side of Spylaw Bank Road, between Dell Road and Pentland Avenue, is the semi-detached house (No. 13) once known as The Bush. A cluster of chimneys, dormers and red-tiled roofs is grouped above the white walls of this early 20th century suburban house which, on its southern side, looks across the site of the former Colinton Station towards the western end of Colinton Dell. In accordance with its date of building, the house and its immediate neighbours were designed under the influence of the Art Nouveau Movement, and The Bush contains a few small Art Nouveau features such as the stained-glass window in the interior.

The interest of this house centres upon its occupant in the early years of the present century, Phoebe Traquair (1852–1936), an artist whose individual style won her international fame during her lifetime, particularly in England, France and America. As so often happened, she remained comparatively unknown for many years in her own country, but today there are clear indications of a reviving interest in the mural paintings with which she decorated the interiors of buildings, several of them in Edinburgh.

Phoebe Anna Moss was born in Dublin but came to Edinburgh on her marriage, in 1873, to Ramsay Traquair, Keeper of the Natural History Department of the Edinburgh Museum of Science and Art. Their elder son, Ramsay R. Traquair (1874–1952) studied under Sir Robert Lorimer and was the architect of several Edinburgh buildings including, in 1910, the former Christian Science Church in Inverleith Terrace. They lived in Dean Park Crescent but moved to The Bush in 1906, the first occupants of the newly built house. She installed a kiln in the long garden at the back for the purpose of jewellery enamelling to which she had turned, along with artistic bookbinding, in addition to embroidery and the mural painting to which she was principally committed.

A gifted and professional artist, she was active at the time when the innovating mind of Patrick Geddes was at work in Edinburgh, and most of her work was inspired by contemporary dissatisfaction with the dreary interiors of Victorian charitable institutions and hospitals, many of which she transformed into more inviting and humanitarian places. Her paintings of angels and children on the walls of the children's mortuary at Rillbank (at the Royal Hospital for Sick Children in Sciennes Road) were aimed at ameliorating the harsh realities of family life among the poor at the end of the 19th century. A feature of her paintings, also used by the Pre-Raphaelite artist Burne-Jones, was the introduction of a black outline around her figures, and this is exemplified in her work at the Song School of St. Mary's Episcopal Cathedral.

It was, however, at the former Catholic Apostolic Church at the corner of Mansefield Place and East London Street that her best-known Edinburgh work of mural decoration was carried out on a grand scale. Here in her representation of scenes from the Old Testament which cover the high walls and ceilings, and which took eight years to complete in 1901, she achieved the climax of her art, and the necessity of painting at great heights for many hours exposed her to considerable danger in the course of their execution. They have been severely damaged by water over a number of years but restoration is likely to take place in the near future. She was the first woman to be made an honorary member of the Royal Scottish

Academy, and examples of her work are to be found in the National Gallery of Scotland, the Royal Museum of Scotland and the Victoria and Albert Museum in London.

Phoebe Traquair's daughter, Hilda, was a distinguished practitioner in the field of embroidery and her second son, Harry, became an eminent ophthalmic surgeon in Edinburgh.

On the corner of Spylaw Avenue and Spylaw Bank Road is SPYLAW BANK HOUSE, a substantial grey-walled 18th century building with its name on the gate-piers at the entrance, which was once the dower-house of the Gillespie estate. Miss F.B. Grahame, the last descendant of John Grahame of Claverhouse, lived in this house. Further east, above the former Colinton branch railway line, is the single-storey, stone-built STATION HOUSE looking southwards and with a little gablet above the door.

An interesting group of houses terminates Spylaw Bank Road at the Colinton end. Two early 19th century single-storey stone cottages are followed by the fortress-like and massive walls of the 18th century house (No. 1 DELL ROAD) on the corner opposite the entrance to Colinton Parish Church.

Cammo House

Within its mature and beautiful grounds, a private estate which has now become a city park, the last remnants can be seen of Cammo House. Built in 1693 by John Menzies, it was purchased from him in 1710 by Sir John Clerk of Penicuik who laid out the park. In 1741 the estate came into the possession of the Watsons of Saughton when it was renamed New Saughton, but it reverted once more to Cammo House on its sale, in 1872, to a brewer called Alexander Campbell who died in 1898. Shortly afterwards it was sold to the Maitland-Tennent family who were the last occupants of the house and who eventually allowed it to deteriorate beyond hope of restoration, and the stabilised surviving walls are all that is left of this once substantial mansion.

Mrs Maitland-Tennent, who brought up her two sons Robert and Percival in the house and was known latterly as the Black Widow of Cammo because of her apparently reclusive habits, became a living legend before her death at the age of ninety-five in 1955. Robert,

The fragmentary remains of Cammo House the grounds of which have been restored as a public park and a habitat for wildlife.

who disliked this lifestyle, had gone to America, but Percival remained, living finally in a caravan while his numerous dogs roamed the park and gained access to the house where they fouled the carpets and wrought havoc on the furniture. On Percival's death in 1975 the damage was compounded by vandalism, theft and fire.

In his will Percival Maitland-Tennent bequeathed the property to The National Trust for Scotland, as recorded on an inscribed plaque on the walls of the ruins. The Trust later, in 1980, feued the estate to what was then the Edinburgh District Council who restored the grounds as a protected habitat for wildlife and a place of public recreation. Conducted walks in the park are organised on a regular basis by the Ranger Service.

It has been claimed that Cammo House was the original of R.L. Stevenson's House of Shaws in his novel *Kidnapped*, but it is likely that that was an amalgam of more than one house, including Cramond (q.v.)

Clerwood

With a portico between two large gables above the windows, Clerwood is a typical Victorian villa built c. 1860 on the east side of Clermiston Road. The home of the Tod family of flour millers before the Second World War, it subsequently became a children's home and is now in commercial ownership. The stables are reached from the same entrance and are in use as a separate property. THE MILL, a 17th century converted mill house, is in Oak Lane at Clermiston.

Colinton Bank House

Above a high wall and standing on high ground opposite Henry Mackenzie's Cottage (q.v.) on the other side of the road is Colinton Bank House, a substantial stone-built villa, while to the east of Henry Mackenzie's Cottage and on the same side of the road is HEATHER COTTAGE, built about 1810 and indicating, by the depth of its gable skews, that it had originally been thatched.

Colinton Castle

The ivy-clad remains of Colinton Castle now stand picturesquely in the grounds of Merchiston Castle School in Colinton Road. Built by the Cunningham family in 1450, it was extended in the 18th century and its present ruinous aspect was engineered in the early 1800s (with the help, says John Geddie, 'of a cannon brought up from Leith') to create a romantic folly. Much demolition had, however, been achieved by Cromwell's soldiery who wrecked the castle in 1650, though restoration work was later carried out.

In 1519 it had been bought, with its estates, by Sir James Foulis, and his descendants lived here until the last decade of the 18th century. One of them, another Sir James, was raised to the bench as Lord Colinton in 1654.

The next owner was Sir William Forbes of Pitsligo, the Edinburgh banker (see George Square and Colinton House), who bought the estate in 1790 and built the elegant Georgian mansion of Colinton House (q.v.) not far from the castle. These two buildings and the grounds surrounding them were acquired by Merchiston Castle School (see Merchiston Castle) in 1925 when the headmaster's house was built beside the castle ruins.

Lord Provost George Drummond (see Drummond Place), a principal initiator of the New Town of Edinburgh, lived in Colinton Castle for some time, and it was the scene of Mrs Oliphant's famous ghost story, *The Open Door*.

Colinton House

As mentioned under Colinton Castle (q.v.), Sir William Forbes of Pitsligo (1739–1806) (see George Square), one of the bankers (his banking house was on the south side of the Parliament Close) who helped to finance the building of the New Town, bought the Colinton estate in 1790 and built a two-storeyed Georgian mansion-house in the grounds, calling it Colinton House. Twin Ionic columns flank the central portico, and single-floor wings extend on either side to create a long, low villa epitomising all the cool, architectural refinement of its period. Sir William died in 1806, before the house was completed, and was followed by his son, also Sir William. The second Sir William Forbes retained his friendship with Sir Walter Scott in spite of his marriage to Williamina Stuart Belsches who would, had Sir Walter been more fortunate, have become Lady Scott.

The Forbes family left Colinton for Edinburgh in 1830, and in 1839 James Abercromby (who in that year became Lord Dunfermline) purchased the estate and house as a retirement residence. He had been appointed Speaker of the House of Commons in 1835 and died at Colinton House at the age of eighty-one. His son Ralph married a daughter of another banking family, the Trotters, to whom the estate then passed (see Swanston Cottage, Mortonhall House and Morton House).

In 1925, the old Napier dwelling of Merchiston Castle (q.v.) proving no longer suitable to the growing and expanding school which had adopted its name, a removal was made to the Colinton estate where a new and larger school, retaining the original name, was built in the grounds.

Colinton House (now known as Gibson House after a former headmaster) was adapted to the needs of a science department and an additional (and regrettable) floor was constructed over the west wing at a later date.

The stable block, the statutory dovecot and an ice house are contemporaneous with the Georgian mansionhouse, and some holly trees from a hedge planted about 1675 are still in existence. The park was laid out by Sir William Forbes.

At Firrhill, near the junction of Colinton Road and Colinton Mains Drive, is FIRRHILL HOUSE, built about 1908, with a Venetian window on the upper floor of the main frontage below a dormer window. It stands among trees and lawns in an extensive garden and was an Old People's Home for a number of years.

Colinton Manse

The 18th century Parish Church of Colinton assumed its present appearance in the early 1900s, but the Manse, which was built in 1783, possibly incorporating part of an older building, has survived, albeit with later alterations. It lies deep in the valley of the Water of Leith where there was always, as Robert Louis Stevenson remembered, 'the sound of water and the sound of mills', while in summer the densely wooded vale brimmed 'like a cup with sunshine and the song of birds'.

The two-storeyed house stands foursquare and plain with prominent chimneys, and bay windows on both floors to the left of the doorway, and, with its paths and lawns, is well enclosed by mature and lofty trees. The Rev. Lewis Balfour, born away to the east in Pilrig House (q.v.) in 1777 and the maternal grandfather of R.L.S., occupied the Manse and the pulpit till his death in 1860. Robert Louis

Colinton Manse, the home of The Rev. Lewis Balfour, grandfather of
R.L.S.

was then just ten years old but he never forgot the house and, above
all, the garden and the river which were so spellbinding to an
imaginative child, where he so often lived and played with his many
cousins – for Lewis Balfour had numerous children – throughout
these carefree summers. Youthful impressions were recalled in the
later, literary years – the dark, cold library where his grandfather 'sat
much alone writing sermons or letters to his scattered family', and
'the long, low dining-room' in which the young Louis played with
building bricks in the 'great open space behind the sofa left entirely
in the shadow'. Outside there was the water-door: 'Down at the
corner of the lawn, next the snuff-mill wall, there was a practicable
passage through the evergreens, and a door in the wall, which let
you out on a small patch of sand, left in the corner by the river. Just
across, the woods rose like a wall into the sky; and their lowest
branches trailed in the black waters.'

Church and Manse have been altered since Stevenson's day, but garden and sylvan stream are, though now bereft of industry, just as he remembered them when he wrote:

> The river, on from mill to mill,
> Flows past our childhood's garden still;
> But ah! we children never more
> Shall watch it from the water-door!

(See Baxter's Place, Howard Place, Heriot Row, Pilrig House and Swanston Cottage.)

Coltbridge House and Cottages

As the 19th century drew to a close a last backward and nostalgic look was cast by its architects (or their clients) to a medieval past with which they sought to identify in stone and lime. Their buildings include the demolished Trinity Cottage (1894) at Goldenacre, the Sir William Fraser Homes (1898) in Spylaw Bank Road (see Peffermill House) and the picturesque almshouse-type Coltbridge Cottages beside the Water of Leith at Roseburn.

The red-roofed, gabled and gableted cottages, with their tall chimney stalks and rustic 'country cottage' aspect, were built in 1894 in accordance with the will of George Pape of Coltbridge House, the donor's tablet on the south gable going on to state that they were for the use of 'three poor widows in all time coming'.

Coltbridge House, beside the Church of the Good Shepherd in Murrayfield Avenue, presents a broad gable (containing a pedimented doorway which looks like a later insertion) to the street, from which it is separated by a long front garden. *Picturesque Notes of an Edinburgh Suburb: Coltbridge, Murrayfield, Roseburn* published by The Murrayfield Residents' Association states that, 'After the Papes, Coltbridge House was occupied briefly by various tenants. . . . From 1874–93 it was occupied by John Herdman of the Edinburgh milling firm of Herdman and Son.' Later 'The house was left to be sold to provide money for the Pape charitable trusts which were administered by the Minister of St. John's Princes Street and St. Cuthbert's and others.'

Coltbridge, at one time a tiny riverside village to the west of Edinburgh, was the scene, in 1745, of the 'Canter of Coltbrig' when Cope's cavalry panicked and fled 'on seeing a few Highland gentlemen', as Grant puts it, 'approach them, mounted, . . . while marching along the old Glasgow Road', not drawing bridle until they reached Prestonpans.

Corstorphine Dower House or Gibson Lodge

Standing in St. Margaret's Park on the south side of Corstorphine High Street is Corstorphine Dower House, built about 1640 by James, Lord Forrester of Corstorphine.

Adam Forrester, a 14th century merchant and Provost of Edinburgh, who lived in Forrester's Wynd near St. Giles in the Old Town, bought the lands of Corstorphine and built the Castle no trace of which, except the doocot and the 15th century sycamore tree, now remains. The carved Forrester effigies, however, still lie in the Parish Church, and the line has not become extinct, being represented today by Lord Verulam (see Gogar Castle).

The Gibsons of Pentland owned the Dower House after the Forresters, and this resulted in its being known also as Gibson Lodge.

This white-harled, T-plan building was originally L-shaped, and crowsteps and a moulded doorway contribute to its picturesque appearance in the park which was laid out in 1927.

To the north of Corstorphine High Street, behind the Glasgow Road at North Gyle, is the restored and modernised former Georgian farmhouse known as GYLE HOUSE, the farm buildings behind it having also been converted for residential use. Gyle House is sheltered by a tall beech hedge and has been enlarged by the 20th century addition of a single-storey eastern extension. It stands in a mature garden, and a lean-to conservatory, entered from the house, is against the west wall.

Corstorphine Hill House

The south side of Corstorphine Hill having been purchased in
1720 by the Edinburgh merchant John Dickie (see Belmont),
part of the ground was sold on his death in 1755 to a brewer called
David Johnstone who, in turn, resold the land to William Keith, an
accountant and a member of the family of Keith of Ravelston (see
Ravelston House), in 1791. The original Corstorphine Hill House
was built by him in 1793. In the second half of the 19th century it
was turned into a Scots Baronial pile which, together with the
grounds, was bought by the Royal Zoological Society of Scotland
in 1912, the last private owner having been a tea merchant with
Melroses of Leith called Macmillan. The red stone turrets and
round towers of this building are still prominent features on its
commanding hillside site.

Now within the precincts of Edinburgh Zoo, Corstorphine Hill House was
built in 1793 and 'baronialised' in the 19th century.

The gates and stone falcons at the Zoo entrance were removed from the house of Falcon Hall at Morningside before its demolition in 1909 and were set up here at a later date (see Burghmuirhead House).

Corstorphine House

Corstorphine House stands in the circus called Corstorphine House Avenue, north-east of Corstorphine High Street, and was constructed in 1832. This plain, two-storey, Georgian villa with bay windows on the ground floor and a later extension to the east was the first of several such houses to be built in Corstorphine, as in other suburban areas of Edinburgh, for the more affluent city-dwellers who wished to have residences in the country. They would appear as a striking contrast to the thatched cottages of old Corstorphine, the last of which were destroyed by fire in 1937.

In 1946 the Corstorphine District Association came into being for the preservation and protection of local amenity and amalgamated with the Corstorphine Trust in 1970.

Craigcrook Castle

The large round tower at Craigcrook Castle indicates an early origin and the woodland trees a secluded site for this historic building. To the 16th-century tower a domestic wing was added in the 17th century and it was further extended by W.H. Playfair in 1835 for Lord Jeffrey (see Duncan's Land and Bonaly Tower).

The house and its environs were well known to Scott. Archibald Constable (1774–1827) (see Atholl Crescent and Trinity Grove), his publisher, lived here for a time, and after him came its most famous occupant, Scott's friend and distinguished contemporary in the Parliament House and later Lord Advocate, Francis Jeffrey (1773–1850), for whom the castle became a loved and much frequented country house. Constable had published, and Jeffrey edited, the *Edinburgh Review*, a periodical of the cutting and thrusting school of literary criticism, Jeffrey himself being a prime example of the fact that, during this golden age in the city's history, Edinburgh bred letters and the law together. He was married twice, his second wife being Miss Wilkes of New York 'for whom, with true gallantry, he ventured across the Atlantic while war was hotly waged between the two countries' in 1813. He died at his townhouse in Moray Place aged 76 (see Bonaly Tower).

The old walls, turrets, tower and crowstepped gables of Craigcrook Castle, its walls in places five feet thick, form a picturesque and pleasing composition, and Lord Cockburn (see Bonaly Tower), well rooted and grounded in the Augustan soil of literary Edinburgh, wrote of it with retrospective nostalgia, 'with the exception of Abbotsford, there were more interesting strangers there than at any other house in Scotland', and Jeffrey himself found infinite relish in getting 'away from courts and crowds' to spend a summer day 'in the luxury of conscious idleness.'

A low modern addition was added to the castle in 1968 when it became for some years the house and offices of an Edinburgh architect (see Buccleuch Place, George Street and Queen Street).

Beside the original entrance in Craigcrook Road is the former Castle Lodge.

Craiglockhart Castle

The ruined fragment of Craiglockhart Castle (or Tower) stands on the south side of Glenlockhart Road not far from its junction with Colinton Road and at the foot of Wester Craiglockhart Hill. This tiny, and probably medieval, towerhouse has an arched doorway, a stair to the upper floor and walls over six feet thick, but its history is obscure and appears to have been unrecorded.

Craiglockhart House

In Craiglockhart Dell Road stands Craiglockhart House, a large building on a corner site built in the 1830s but with later alterations. The entrance, on one side, is in a rounded projection and the windows contain Gothic glazing which, with other details, gives the house a vaguely neo-Gothick appearance. It is surrounded by an extensive garden, suburban housing having spread across most of the original grounds. The former Lodge, a stone-built, single-storey house with label mouldings above the windows and now a veterinary surgery, lies behind railings on the north side of the Dell Inn in Lanark Road (see Slateford).

Cramond House

The plain, traditionally Scottish central portion of Cramond House, off Cramond Glebe Road, was built in the 1680s by the descendants of James Inglis of Cramond Tower (q.v.) as a more

Cramond House, standing among the excavated foundations of a Roman fort, is of several building periods and now belongs to Cramond Church.

Old buildings at Cockle Mill, beside the River Almond, which have been converted into 20th-century houses.

modern, fashionable and convenient place of abode. To make room for the house, and to provide the required space around it on which to lay out secluded grounds, the cottages and other rural buildings which had grown up beside the medieval Tower were taken down and a new Georgian 'planned village' was created during the 18th century a short distance away. This included, after the middle of the century, the two-storeyed, white-harled SCHOOLHOUSE (serving as a schoolmaster's house and school), with astragaled windows and gable chimney stacks, which still stands on the west side of Cramond Glebe Road.

Additions to the front and back of Cramond House were made in 1772 and at later dates in the 18th century, tall round-headed Georgian windows now making their appearance, thus enhancing the status-symbolism of the house. Further additions were made in the following century when it was owned by the Craigie-Halkett family, descendants of James Inglis who had acquired the original property in 1622.

In one of the galleries of Cramond Parish Church can be seen, wrote John Geddie in the 1920s, 'the chair occupied by Queen Victoria on a visit to her mother, the Duchess of Kent, who was for three years a tenant of Cramond House'. The mansion now belongs to the Church, itself a historic building, and the Queen's bedroom when staying with her mother has been incorporated in the church officer's flat. The house can therefore claim without question to have been slept in by Queen Victoria even if its identification with Stevenson's House of Shaws has been frequently disputed, especially with Cammo House (q.v.).

CRAMOND MANSE, also in Cramond Glebe Road and nearly out of sight within its garden, was built in 1745 but has extensive mid-19th century additions carried out by the Victorian architect, David Bryce.

In the late 18th and early 19th centuries there existed a miniature black country along the banks of the River Almond, which like the Water of Leith was made to work for the community, its waterpower driving the iron and other mills that grew up along its length. Houses were built beside the mills for the mill hands and their employers, the latter being exemplified in the high-standing, 18th century COCKLE MILL MANAGER'S HOUSE. Entered from Whitehouse Road, it is only from the lower level at the back that it can be seen to look down like a watch-tower (which indeed it was) on the workers in the milling area below. The office building from which Cockle Mill was administered has survived and has been converted into attractive 20th century housing.

The workers' cottages in Cadell Row, called after the family who owned the mills (see Cadell House), have also been modernised and are now desirable suburban houses in an interesting environment.

Further upriver towards the Old Cramond Brig a few two-storeyed cottages line the pathway at the site of Dowie's Mill. Here too is the quaint little pantile-roofed PRIMROSE COTTAGE standing, demurely as its namesake, among woodland trees and backing into the embankment opposite the Almond. The cottage that once served as a toll-house from the opening years of the 19th century is at the east end of the old bridge, a turnpike road once running here on the banks of the river. Here also, and both white-harled, are the two other houses of HAUGH PARK and WILLOWBANK.

Cramond Tower

A long the banks of the little River Almond, in the angle created by the stream and the sea, the village of Cramond, its boats and its buildings alike attractive to all who visit it, stands alone in its possession of visible evidence of a historic past that goes back through different periods of development to the days of the Roman legions and their roads and forts. One of the earliest Roman settlements in Scotland, its former existence is now demonstrated on the ground at several excavated sites.

Cramond's oldest building to survive in reasonable preservation is its 15th century Tower, owned and occupied by the Bishops of Dunkeld in consequence of a Royal grant enabling them more conveniently to make periodic visits to the Abbey on Inchcolm which fell within their jurisdiction. In 1622 the old structure passed to James Inglis, an Edinburgh merchant, who used the Tower as his house and whose descendants became the hereditary lairds of Cramond. In the later years of the 17th century the medieval building became outdated and the family followed the dictates of fashion by erecting Cramond House (q.v.) on the new manorhouse principle. Fortunately for the future of the village with its historical continuity, they were not disposed to knock down their ancestral home and, whatever else may have crumbled into dust, the old Tower survived, ruinous but undemolished among the rosebay willow-herb, and has now been restored to its full original height as a dwellinghouse within a little landscaped garden.

Dalry House

B y the middle of the 17th century fortification was no longer the principal requirement of the builders of substantial houses, and in 1661, as recorded within on a plaster ceiling on the first floor decorated with the initials of Charles II and a crowned saltire, Dalry House, which had been built by Thomas Mudie in the early years of the century, was changed into a more domesticated manorhouse. Its white-harled walls and projecting stair-towers with ogee roofs, one dating from the 17th century and the other from the 18th, tell a story of more settled times, a historical fact which is not borne out by the recorded accounts of the Chiesley family into whose possession it came in the second half of the 17th century. Dalry Manor House had hardly stood in peace for twenty years before John Chiesley, the son of Walter Chiesley, a prosperous Edinburgh merchant, complained to the Privy Council that he and his servants had been beaten and wounded in his own house and his horses turned out of their stables by some 'gentlemen of the Royal Life Guards' who had committed the old Scots crime of 'hamesucken'. They themselves, however, were no better. In 1689 Sir George Lockhart of Carnwath, the Lord President of the Court of Session, was shot outside his house in the Old Bank Close by John Chiesley of Dalry because of a legal disagreement and in a fit of what appears to have been hereditary temper, and the rough justice of the time was summarily administered. Chiesley's right hand, having held the lethal weapon, was cut off before his execution and his body, after being hung in chains, was taken in stealth by his relations to a secret burial. But peace was not restored to Dalry House. The unquiet spirit of its late occupant was soon revisiting its earthly mansion, particularly that part of it which opened towards the garden at the back. Years later when a garden wall was being repaired a stone seat which stood beside it required to be removed. A grave was revealed beneath and there seemed little doubt that it was that of Chiesley of Dalry as the right arm of the skeletal body had been shortened by a hand. After this discovery the haunting of the old manorhouse was said to have mysteriously ceased.

The Chiesley tenure came to an end in 1696 when the property passed to Sir Alexander Brand, a merchant, who changed the name to Brandfield House (although it reverted to the old name of Dalry at the conclusion of the Brand occupation). Sir Alexander was a shrewd but unscrupulous business operator and, when high-risk commercial undertakings resulted in serious financial loss, he decided on an unusual method of solving his problems. In 1706 he advertised in the *Edinburgh Evening Courant* that he intended to raffle his house and offered £5 tickets to all who might be interested in buying a mansion (and its contents) at such a knock-down price. This does not appear to have produced the enthusiastic response he had presumably expected as, for whatever reason, the scheme was abandoned and the estate was eventually feued for building purposes, the whole area in time becoming industrialised. Later occupants were members of the Walker family of Old Coates House (q.v.) and the students of an Episcopal Ladies' Training College for which purpose the house had been taken over in the early 20th century.

Dalry House, in Orwell Place, now belongs to the Edinburgh and Leith Old People's Welfare Council by whom it has been used as a Day Centre since 1968. The building itself was restored in 1963.

The old meaning of Dalry was 'the king's vale', and this may be compared with that of Croft-an-Righ (q.v.), or 'the king's croft' near Holyrood Palace.

In Distillery Lane (off Dalry Road near Haymarket), so called from the Caledonian Distillery built here in 1855, is EASTER DALRY HOUSE. Originally an elegant little 18th-century mansionhouse overlooking a garden on the north side, the former attractions of its environment have been obliterated. It has two storeys, and the ball finials on either side of the present north entrance are half buried in the wall. On the south elevation a Venetian window, the large central light filled in, in the middle of the upper floor has an acutely pointed gablet, crowned by a chimney stalk, immediately above. There are also tiny, single-storey wings to east and west. The house is still in use but as commercial premises.

In 1711 the eastern half of the lands of Dalry, called the 'Town' of Dalry, with the manor place, houses and 147 acres of arable land were sold to John Watson, younger, an Edinburgh merchant. The 'manor place' is, however, too early to be the present Easter Dalry House which may have been built on the site of a previous dwelling.

Deanhouse

R estored in 1996 as three separate flats, Deanhouse dates from the 18th century, although the top floor is later, and is situated in Damside in the Dean Village, an application by a firm of builders for its demolition in 1988 having been refused. Two small modern houses have been built beside it.

Easter Park

Although Easter Park, off Barnton Avenue, looks in all respects like a little Georgian mansion, it was in fact built, by the tea-merchant family of Melrose (see Chapel House), as late as 1905 in a style closely resembling the work of the Adam brothers. The house and ten-acre estate belonged latterly to the Youngers and were sold to a property developer on the death of the last Younger occupant about 1971. The parkland environment of the villa beside Bruntsfield Golf Course and not far from the sea was thereafter built up with modern housing, the house itself (including its marble mantelpieces) being spared and converted into flats.

Easter Park has a projecting portico on the main frontage and a delicately ornamented frieze below the roofline.

A reproduction Adamesque villa of 1905, Easter Park is now surrounded by suburban housing.

Fernielaw

At Fernielaw Avenue, in Colinton, is the house called Fernielaw. Built in the mid-18th century, it is a plain, harled building with a Venetian window on the upper floor. A small crowstepped addition at the north-west was made about 1850, and a semi-octagonal porch and oriel window were added to the south front. The house was reconstructed in the 20th century when it gained a west wing of two storeys and an attic.

Fernielaw was originally a farmhouse, and the old driveway to the house and farm is now Fernielaw Avenue.

Gogar Castle usually called Castle Gogar

The fine baronial mansionhouse of Gogar, having witnessed many changes across the years in its environment, stands north of the Glasgow Road at the edge of Edinburgh Airport at Turnhouse.

The parish of Gogar was owned by the monks of Holyrood before passing to Sir John Forrester of Corstorphine (see Corstorphine Dower House) in the early 15th century. A hundred years later it belonged to the Logans of Restalrig (see Lochend House) and came eventually into the possession of Sir John Cowper, a Lord Ordinary of the Court of Session, who built the castle in 1625, the estate having been purchased by his father in 1601. Sir John placed the date, his inititals and those of Harriet Sinclair, his wife, on a round-headed dormer window pediment. The main, semi-octagonal stair-tower in the re-entrant angle of this L-plan house has been corbelled out to the square where the flat roof is enclosed by a Renaissance balustrade combining the functions of a balcony and a look-out point. This castle-cum-manorhouse displays features from both its lawless and its more law-abiding past and has a great hall above barrel-vaulted cellars, the cellars having been converted into a spacious entrance hall. There are gunports in the round, corbelled turrets of the four-storey building, and the waters of the Gogar Burn flow through the grounds.

Gogarbank House

With the Gogar Burn running through its grounds, the ivy-covered walls of Gogarbank House stand near the National Trust for Scotland garden at Suntrap behind the Glasgow Road. Two shallow wings flank a two-storeyed central block which, with a small columned porch, was built in 1800. The house and its beautiful walled and terraced garden belong to the Ministry of Defence and are used as a residence for the G.O.C. Scotland.

Gogarbank House, beside the Gogar Burn, was built in 1800.

Hailes House

Sir James Clerk of Penicuik was the builder of Hailes House, now in Hailes Avenue at Kingsknowe, about 1760. This rather unimpressive Georgian building of three storeys has a little stairway to the entrance on the first floor and chimney stacks that rise from scrolled stonework on either side of the house. The red roof with awkward-looking dormer windows is an unfortunate Edwardian 'improvement'.

For many years Hailes House did service as a youth hostel and later, for a time, as an hotel.

Henry Mackenzie's Cottage

A little derelict cottage by the roadside, at what used to be the Colinton tram terminus just before the descent into Colinton Village, its chimneys rising above the green mass of low trees and bushes by which it was almost overwhelmed, was rebuilt in 1996 and is now occupied by a firm of architects. A plaque on the railings beside the pavement inscribed: 'In this house lived Henry Mackenzie, author of *The Man of Feeling*, Born 25th August 1745, Died 13th January 1831', has been relocated on the outside wall of the cottage.

In 1804, on the recommendation of Lord Melville, Henry Mackenzie was appointed Comptroller of the Tax Office which was then situated at No. 84 Princes Street. He edited the literary magazines *The Lounger* and *The Mirror*, in consequence of which he was called the 'Northern Addison' by Scott, and was also a contributor to *Blackwood's Magazine*. *The Man of Feeling* became much the best known of his works and was sometimes used as a name for the author himself.

During the years 1795 to 1807 Mackenzie occupied as tenant the charming little Midlothian house of Auchindinny, designed by Sir William Bruce, in the village of that name where a print of the writer hung on the walls. Renowned for his wit and conversation, Henry Mackenzie spent the last years of his long life, when he was not at his Colinton cottage, at No. 6 Heriot Row (see Belmont).

Henry Mackenzie's Cottage, No. 302 Colinton Road. Unoccupied for many years, it was rebuilt as offices in 1996.

Hillwood House

A large, 33-roomed, Scots Baronial mansion with a massive, round and battlemented tower above a neo-Gothick entrance porch, Hillwood House stands on the west side of Corstorphine Hill between Clermiston and Cairnmuir Roads. It was built about 1870 by MacGibbon and Ross, two architects now better known for their treatise on *The Castellated and Domestic Architecture of Scotland*.

Hillwood House, by then in the ownership of Edinburgh Corporation, as it was known at that time, and in a state of serious deterioration, was the subject of prolonged controversy in the late 1960s when it was sold by the Council for £4000 ostensibly on condition that it remained a single dwellinghouse and that the extensively wooded grounds would not be exploited by the purchaser, who was in fact a member of the Council and who appeared to be so exploiting them, for timber.

Prior to the Second World War the house and its estate were the property of an official of the Drambuie Liqueur Co. Ltd.

Kirkbrae House

High above the Water of Leith and at the south end of the Dean Bridge, is a much altered and extended house which was planted on the clifftop more than fifty years before Thomas Telford, the bridge-builder, had been born. In its early life the house was something of an inn or place of refreshment, particularly for the baxters, or bakers, whose mills and granaries were lower down beside the river, and was a plain, crowstepped building typical of the late 17th century. It is now No. 10 Randolph Cliff.

For short periods in the mid-19th century it was occupied first by the sculptor William Brodie, R.S.A., and then by his fellow-sculptor John Hutchison, R.S.A., but it was their successor who gave Kirkbrae House the much more baronial and extravagant appearance which it has today. This was a cab-hirer named James Stewart who took possession in 1860 and, living to the age of eighty-seven, died in the house in 1917. His coach house, now restored to accommodate an architectural practice, can be seen in Bell's Brae. Stewart was 'a patriarchal figure seated in tall hat and Inverness-cape outside his door at the end of the Bridge' and was a well-known Edinburgh character.

To begin with he contended himself with adding neo-Gothick details, including some carved and ornamented stones from other buildings, to the existing structure, but in 1890 he called in the architect J. Graham Fairley considerably to enlarge the house. The problems created by its precipitous site having been overcome, a latter-day towerhouse was constructed, between the old building and the Dean Bridge, which can be seen to greatest effect from the path beside the river. Among the interior embellishments were red pine panelling and friezes inscribed with Biblical quotations.

In more recent years the house was sub-divided to facilitate the introduction of commercial enterprise. It has since, however, been fully restored to domestic occupation and a separate flat has been created in part of the Stewart extension. The history of this house was written by the late Basil Skinner in 1982.

In the Dean Village, overlooking the Water of Leith, the early 19th century WEST MILL affords a good example of the conversion of an old industrial building to residential use. Twenty-two flats were created within the mill in 1973 for the Link Housing Association. The old BELL'S MILLS HOUSE and BELL'S BRAE HOUSE are nearby.

Lammerburn

This is a house distinguished primarily by the novelty of its ornamental exterior walls, gables and even chimney stalks, where a rustic effect has been achieved by the use of light and dark brown patterned stonework. It was built in 1859 at No. 10 Napier Road, the architect being Sir James Gowans (see Waverley House) who had just designed for himself the fantastic, pagoda-topped Rockville on the opposite side of the street at No. 3. A thirty-roomed mansion which proved difficult to adapt for alternative purposes, Rockville was demolished in 1965.

Gowans, who was also an engineer, was Dean of Guild in Edinburgh and was the architect of The New Edinburgh Theatre, which later became the Synod Hall, in Castle Terrace. Built in 1875, it suffered the same fate as Rockville, both buildings being demolished within a year of each other.

Sir James pioneered the modular system of proportion, Lammerburn being a good example, which was later taken up by many modern architects.

Lauriston Castle

Between the years 1590 and 1827 Lauriston Castle, in Cramond Road North, consisted of the square, three-storeyed tower with two corbelled turrets at the south-west corner of the present building and its estate extended from the shoreline of the Firth of Forth to Davidson's Mains. The name of Lauriston can be traced back to the early 14th century when the area is mentioned in a charter as 'the lands of Lourestoun'.

At the beginning of the 17th century the property belonged to Alexander Napier, the brother of John Napier, the inventor of logarithms (see Merchiston Castle), whose father, Sir Archibald, most probably built, and certainly occupied, the old keep. But it was in the late 17th and early 18th centuries that the meteoric career of its most famous owner, John Law of Lauriston (1671–1729), who is said to have been born in the tower, made its mark on Scotland's history and, indeed, on that of France as well. He was, says John Geddie, a financial genius who plunged into 'wildly ambitious schemes that ended in his ruin and almost in the ruin of France.' It was William Law, his father, a goldsmith and banker in Edinburgh, who bought the castle in 1683, and in 1720 his son became Comptroller-General of France to Louis XV. John Law's exploitation of undeveloped territories, a scheme that became known as the 'Mississippi System', was at first successful, but only a few months after his appointment the notes issued by his bank, which had been established in 1716, were declared to be of no value and, says James Grant, he 'fled from the scenes of his splendour and disgrace, and after wandering through various countries, died in poverty at Venice on the 21st of March 1729.'

In 1823 the castle was acquired from the Law descendants by the Edinburgh banker and proprietor of the *Caledonian Mercury* newspaper, Thomas Allan, who employed the architect William Burn (1789–1870) to make extensive additions to the old structure. The building remains largely as Burn designed it – a keep and a Victorian house in mutual harmony – although a library floor was added about 1875.

Lauriston Castle entered upon the final stage of its private ownership when William Robert Reid (1854–1919), a specialist in interior design, took possession in 1902. He installed bathrooms and central heating, redecorated the building in the style which can be seen today and restored the grounds and gardens to the high standard which has since been maintained.

W.R. Reid and his wife brought their fine collection of period furniture and other works of art to Lauriston. Of particular interest are more than one hundred pieces of the rare 'Blue John' ware created from the fluorspar mined in the Derbyshire Peak District during the 18th and 19th centuries.

After the death of Mrs Reid in 1926 the castle and its grounds became the property of the nation in terms of their joint will and have since then been open to the public as a unique example of late Victorian and Edwardian taste.

Laverockdale

Sir Robert Lorimer (1864–1929), who has been described as the most brilliant Scottish architect of his time, worked mainly in the vernacular tradition, producing what might be called an original, early 20th century Scots Baronial style which is exemplified in Laverockdale, in Dreghorn Loan at Colinton, erected immediately

The mansionhouse of Laverockdale which was built in a traditional Scottish style by Sir Robert Lorimer in 1912–14.

before the First World War but harking back to the solid, stone-built houses of 17th century Scotland. It is a high, severe building with a central stair-tower and in complete contrast to the many cottage-type dwellings he designed in Edinburgh, those for which he is most widely known being also in Colinton and characterised by the abandonment of straight lines and acute angles in favour of gently curving roofs and gables. His little row of seven such houses called RUSTIC COTTAGES at the west end of Colinton Road were built in the early 1900s and form a charming group.

At Laverockdale, which has been sub-divided into two separate houses, Lorimer also built a stable block, entered through an arched courtyard, and a two-storey, crowstep-gabled Lodge House with steep roof and pedimented semi-dormer windows which has now become a dwellinghouse in its own right. Also located in the extensive garden area was a large 'Dutch barn' which is thought to have been one of several hunting lodges in the Pentland Hills. A new house, called The Dutch Barn and built to resemble the original, now occupies the site.

25 Learmonth Terrace

'The final west section' of Learmonth Terrace, says *The Buildings of Scotland: Edinburgh*, 'did not get beyond No. 25, a house so grandiose that no-one could hope to follow it' and it describes the interior as 'the most sumptuous in the city.' Since 1925 the headquarters of the Royal Auxiliary Air Force, it was designed by the Leith architect James Simpson in 1891 for the wealthy wine and whisky merchant Arthur Sanderson (1846–1915) who wished to display his notable art collection to best advantage. The interior decorator was W. Scott Morton, well-known for his work in the field of church furnishing.

Sanderson's business suffered as a result of First World War restrictions and shortly before his death it collapsed with the loss of his entire fortune, his old master paintings and collection of period furniture being sold and the proceeds used to pay his creditors.

The interior with its ornate woodcarving and elaborate ceilings has been magnificently restored by the RAuxAF, including the gold and mosaic ceiling of the entrance hall. The staircase with its carved winged horses is surmounted by figures of Athena and Hera and above is a representation of a Parthenon frieze. Scott Morton's own invention of Tynecastle canvas, which can be moulded to reproduce carving or plasterwork, was used to brilliant effect in the house, especially in the Parthenon frieze, and the billiard room has intricate oak carving in a neo-Elizabethan style.

Main Point House

The junction of three streets, Bread Street, East Fountainbridge and High Riggs, outside the western limits of the Old Town, is known as Main Point and this name has been placed beside the street names to recall the area's identity in the 19th century. The 18th century Main Point House is described by Mary MacDonald in *By the Three Great Roads* which records the history of Tollcross, Fountainbridge and the West Port. 'The house', she writes, 'still existing at the Main Point, No. 4 High Riggs, occupied on the ground floor by the Burke and Hare Bar, was built in 1770 with an elegant facade. It was described as a "gusset house", which aptly indicated its important position at the point of a triangle with main roads on either side.'

This house, the ground-floor shop becoming a public house in 1897, has had a number of detrimental alterations but has escaped the almost total demolition and ongoing rebuilding of High Riggs which runs up to Main point from Tollcross.

Marchfield

This most attractive Georgian house, built between 1810 and 1813, has two floors and a dormer-windowed attic storey, a Doric-pilastered porch with frieze and cornice and, above it, a round-headed niche containing a statue on a pedestal. Above both ends of the building rise large chimney stacks having within their bases openings similar to the central niche (and having the same round, ornamented heads) which serve as additional attic windows. There is a semicircular bow at the back of the house and single-storey, set back wings extend on either side.

Marchfield was occupied by John Donaldson, Professor of Music at Edinburgh University in the mid-19th century, and was the home of Sir Andrew Murray, Lord Provost of the city, in the mid-20th.

To the south is a stable block with crowstepped gables and pigeon entrances in the slopong roof. These surviving buildings stand on the north side of Hillhouse Road, near Davidson's Mains, although part of the grounds has been built over.

Merchiston Castle

The stout old tower of Merchiston Castle looks peaceful now in its latter-day educational role as part of Napier University, but it has witnessed strange and stirring times throughout its long history.

The square, L-plan tower with corbelled battlements, tall chimney stacks and cap-house was built on the western edge of the Burgh Muir. It was surrounded by a moat and had, it is alleged, a secret passage providing, when need arose, an escape route to the north. Exactly when and by whom it was erected are not known but it passed to Alexander Napier, ancestor of the Lords Napier and Ettrick, who was Lord Provost of Edinburgh in 1438 and who was known as Napier of Merchiston (see Lauriston Castle). His son, Sir Alexander, was also Lord Provost at a later date as well as one of James II's ambassadors in Europe. The fifth Sir Alexander fell at Flodden with James IV.

It was not until the middle of the 16th century that the castle's most famous occupant was born. Sir Archibald Napier of Merchiston, later Master of the Mint to James VI, was only sixteen when his son John Napier (1550–1617) was born fourteen years before Galileo and one year, says Grant, 'after John Knox had been released from the French galleys'. 'His mother was Janet, only daughter of Sir Francis Bothwell, and sister of Adam, Bishop of Orkney.' John was possessed of an insatiable thirst for knowledge. 'He applied himself closely to the study of mathematics, and it is conjectured that he gained a taste for that branch of learning during his residence . . . in Italy' where 'he escaped some perils that existed at

The old Napier stronghold of Merchiston Tower has been restored within the complex of Napier University in Colinton Road.

home.' A visitation of the plague had placed the family in especial danger because of the proximity of the castle to the Burgh Muir 'where the infected were driven out to grovel and die, under the very walls of Merchiston'.

Returning home, John Napier's pursuit of learning was rudely interrupted when, in the early 1570s, the old fortalice became the scene of desperate fighting when 'the savage Douglas wars surged wildly round its walls'. As he did not actively support the Queen's party in the struggle for power in Scotland after Mary's flight to England, he was imprisoned in Edinburgh Castle. It was garrisoned by Kirkcaldy of Grange who a short time before had turned his 'iron guns' on Merchiston because 'certain soldiers of the King's party occupied it. . . . The solitary tower formed the key of the southern approach to the city; thus, whoever triumphed, it became the object of the opponent's enmity.'

On his release from captivity John Napier left Edinburgh, but the King's men garrisoned his castle and on the 5th of May 1572 the Queen's troops besieged it. Storming the outworks and setting fire to them, the 'hard struggle' seemed to be going in their favour until 'a body of the King's men came from Leith in hot haste, and compelled the assailents to retire.' Another attack was made on 10th June under the Earl of Huntly but it ended in confusion and the earl's horse was subsequently 'killed under him by a shot from Holyrood Palace'.

More conflict was to come, though of a different nature. A shortage of food was one of the consequences of the civil strife, and foraging parties set out in search of well-stocked fields. Oxen and other 'spoil' were taken from the Napier lands and a clash of arms took place on one occasion when the predators, 'whom hunger had rendered desperate', got the better of their pursuers.

'When peace came the philosopher returned to his ancestral tower' and its battlements became the observatory from which he now turned his eyes towards the heavens as an astrologer. He was presumed 'by the vulgar of his time' to possess mysterious powers and to exercise them with the assistance of a familiar in the shape of a jet-black cock, a reputation which he did nothing to discourage. Today, however, he is best remembered for his invention of logarithms which he presented to the world in a book brought out in 1614. It was 'a discovery which made him famous all over Europe'. By then he was near the end of his life and died three years later in his 'ancient tower of Merchiston'. Passing to his descendants, it became the residence, during college vacations, of the Marquis of Montrose (1612–50) (see Moray House), whose guardian and brother-in-law was Lord Napier.

Still owned by the Lords Napier and Ettrick, the castle became, in 1833, the location of Merchiston Castle School which was founded by Charles Chalmers, the brother of Dr Thomas Chalmers (see Westgate House), after which additions were made to the original building. It was not until 1930, the estate of Colinton House (q.v.) further to the west in Colinton Road having been purchased five years earlier, that the old history-haunted tower was vacated and left, silent and mouldering, to contemplate its turbulent past.

Thirty years later new life returned. Restored and stripped of its Victorian additions, the astrologer's tower once more stood foresquare and unencumbered, but this time as the focal building of the Napier College of Commerce and Technology (now Napier University) which was built around two open-plan quadrangles. A fixed outside stair climbs to the original first floor entrance and in the original hall a Charles II carved plaster ceiling can still be seen. A splendid painted timber ceiling dated 1581 was brought from Preston Grange House near Prestonpans and installed in the present Board Room. Outside, the lion-surmounted gateway was constructed, from older stones, in the 19th century.

No. 16 Colinton Road is the steep-roofed, bay-windowed MER-CHISTON COTTAGE which, with its single, southward-looking, pedimented dormer window, is partly concealed behind a hedge. It was built, for the Bursar of Merchiston Castle School, in 1846.

Murrayfield House

The lands of Inverleith originally stretched as far west as the location of Murrayfield House, but on the Nisbets of Dean (see Craigentinny House) acquiring that ground it became known as Nisbet's Parks. The house itself is an early Georgian laird's dwelling with harled rubble walls in the heart of Murrayfield, built, on the site of an earlier house, in 1735 by a later proprietor, the advocate Archibald Murray of the Cringletie family of that name near Peebles. A tall block of three-storeys rises from a pedimented doorway to a pediment-shaped feature at the roof-line, surmounted by an urn at each of the three angles, which frames a Venetian window on the upper floor. On the east side is a lower wing added about 1780 by Lord Henderland who died before the corresponding wing on the other side could be constructed, thus detracting from the overall symmetry. Archibald Murray's son, Alexander, who was born in 1736 and was raised to the bench as Lord Henderland, died of cholera in Murrayfield House in 1795. It is from this family that the district takes its name. Inside the house the wood-panelled dining-room was enlarged and the new walls covered with a plaster replica of the original panelling, the difference between them being undetectable.

In the early 20th century a proposal to extend Murrayfield Avenue to the north was threatening the demolition of Murrayfield House which was saved by the vigorous protests of a niece of Dr Thomas Chalmers (see Westgate House) who was then living in the house. Its route was consequently led around the house and its gardens as can be clearly seen today in the awkward angles taken by the road at this point.

Ravelston House

The original 17th century house of Ravelston, built to a Z-plan design for defence by firearms, was largely destroyed by fire in the early 19th century. The stair-tower, however, remains as a reminder of the older building which was put up by Sir George Foulis, his initials and those of his wife being recorded over the doorway together with the date 1622. George Foulis, who was a bailie of the City of Edinburgh and Master of the King's Mint, died in 1633, but his descendants forfeited the estate after the 1745 Rebellion.

The present house was built a short distance away by Alexander Keith who had acquired the lands of Ravelston about 1790 (see Corstorphine Hill House). It has an elegant stone stair leading to the entrance on the ground floor above a half-sunk basement, and a three-storey central tower, one storey higher than the rest of the building, which terminates in a pyramidal roof with urns and a slender, crowning finial.

Alexander Keith, Knight-Marischal of Scotland, was created a baronet by George IV during his visit to Edinburgh in 1822, at which time the townhouse of the Keiths was No. 43 Queen Street. A frequent visitor who enjoyed the company and conversation of Mrs Murray Keith to whom he was related was Sir Walter Scott. The last owners were the Stewart-Clarks, and when the house was finally left unoccupied about 1960 it was bought, together with the estate, by the Edinburgh Merchant Company.

The walled garden at Ravelston, with its long herbaceous borders, grass paths and ancient Cedar of Lebanon, was probably created by the Foulis family for the original house and was an outstanding example of a period garden that was still in an excellent state of preservation. By 1967 new buildings for The Mary Erskine School had been constructed beside Ravelston House, which has been retained, but no trace remains of the beautiful old garden.

An interesting survivor from the time of the old Ravelston House is the 17th century double lectern doocot. Its walls over three feet thick, more than two thousand birds had been able to nest inside. A stone pigeon-bath, the only Scottish example so far to be recorded, was discovered inside. In 1974 the Ravelston doocot was extended, using the stones taken from the nesting boxes, and converted to a cottage, the lantern openings for the birds and their corbelled vaulting forming a highly unusual ceiling on the upper floor. The extension provides space for an entrance hall, a kitchen and a staircase.

RAVELSTON LODGE, No. 195 Queensferry Road, at the Blackhall entrance to the former Ravelston House grounds, stands just within the gates and was built about the beginning of the 20th century. More roof than wall, this little cottage has a long and steeply sloping gable on the eastern side from the centre of which rises a tall chimney stalk, the windowed upper part of the gable and two dormer windows in the roof beyond it indicating living space on the higher level.

Redford House

Redford House in Redford Road is a large, white-harled building with a curved frontage which has had quite a number of later additions. Constructed for Lord Redford about 1700, it has now been sub-divided for residential purposes.

A later owner of the house, R.A. Macfie of Dreghorn, re-erected part of the huge attic storey of William Adam's Old Royal Infirmary of 1738, which was demolished in 1884, as a stable block inside the gates. Known as the DRUMMOND SCROLLS, this very ornate architectural relic, with a small triangular pediment above Roman Ionic pilasters in the centre, and massive scrolls with elaborate leaf and flower carving, on the southern side, is a surprising feature which is, however, largely hidden from view by a wooden paling. The Covenanters' Monument, also in Redford Road, is the work of Macfie of Dreghorn as well and consists of four Roman Ionic columns from the Old Infirmary. It was erected at the same time as the Drummond Scrolls.

Redford House, built in 1700, has been divided into separate dwelling-houses.

Beside the monument is the entrance to the Ministry of Defence buildings on the site of the demolished Dreghorn Castle. The lands, originally known as Dregern, belonged to the family of Foulis of Colinton in the 16th century. In 1671 they passed by marriage to Sir William Murray, Master of Works to Charles II, who is thought to have built a house or 'manor place', parts of which survived within the later building until recent years. The advocate John Maclaurin, a son of Colin Maclaurin, Professor of Mathematics at Edinburgh University and later Lord Dreghorn, acquired the property in 1763.

The last private owners of Dreghorn Castle were Robert Andrew Macfie, a Liverpool merchant who afterwards became Member of

Parliament for Leith Burghs for some years, and his son. R.A. Macfie purchased the castle in 1862 and died in 1893. In 1905 part of the estate was bought by the War Department for the purpose of building Cavalry and Infantry Barracks. Finally, in 1913, the castle and the remaining grounds were purchased by them from the Macfie trustees.

Redhall House

The present house at the western end of Craiglockhart Drive South is the second building on the lands known from at least as early as the 13th century as Redhall or, as it was anciently written, Reidhall. Edward I of England, according to Grant, 'is said to have been at Redhall in the August of 1298'.

The fortalices of Colinton and Redhall figured in Cromwell's mid-17th century invasion of Scotland when they were stormed by General Monk's Regiment which later became the Coldstream Guards. Between the English defeat at Leith and their subsequent victory at Dunbar, Redhall Castle fell to the forces led by Monk who laid siege to it in August 1650.

The old house belonged to Sir Adam Otterburn (a name still preserved in nearby Otterburn Park), Lord Advocate during the reign of James V and whose townhouse was in the High Street. He was Provost of the city at the time of the 'Rough Wooing', and when he tried unsuccessfully to negotiate with Hertford, who would accept nothing less than unconditional surrender and the handing over of the infant Queen, ' 'twere better', said Sir Adam, 'that the city should stand to its defence'. The citizens, carrying the Blue Blanket, were under arms and Otterburn galloped back to place himself at their head. Hertford retreated a few days later, but only after the Old Town had been burned and ravaged, the smoke of the blazing timber-fronted houses helping to drive out the surviving remnant of the invading army. Sir Adam was one of the most enlightened men of his time and was Provost on several occasions. He had the unfortunate distinction, however, of being the only holder of that office to be assassinated, being killed by one of the Earl of Arran's servants in 1547.

A fine old hexagonal doocot of 1756, still standing near the castle

Millbank – a splendid early 18th century house in Redhall Bank Road.

site and built of the same red stone, is ornamented with a shield bearing the Otterburn coat-of-arms.

The oldest part of the later manorhouse, today bricked up and deserted beside two modern school buildings, is partly composed of some original 'reid' stones from the old fortalice. It was built in 1758, a pleasant but rather ponderous mansion with early 20th century extensions including the prominent portico with a pediment flanked by two classical urns above it at roof level. Captain John Inglis, who took heroic part in the victorious Battle of Camperdown in 1797, was a member of the family who built the present house and in whose possession it remained until well into the 20th century.

On the other side of the Water of Leith, in Redhall Bank Road, is the charming, rubble-built MILLBANK, built c. 1700, with a circular window in the central pediment. It is flanked by lower, single-storey wings, each with white walls and red-pantiled roof. Not far from the site of Boag's Mill, one of many on the banks of the river, Millbank was once a coaching inn.

Roseburn House

This very ancient house near the Water of Leith in Murrayfield has been described by James Grant as small, quaint and massive 'with crowstepped gables and great chimneys'. Two lintel stones with dates and inscriptions have been incorporated in the walls and Grant gives English translations of two of them: 'When you will enter at Christ his Door 1562' and 'Aye mind you the room to the poor'. An even earlier date, 1526, appears along with the legend 'God keip oure crowne, and send gude succession'. The ground floor 'is strongly vaulted with massive stone'. Why the house should display the Royal Arms on a courtyard wall is not known, although tradition 'associated it with the presence there of Mary and Bothwell', and one of the apartments is called 'Queen Mary's room'. More

Roseburn House which belonged to Mungo Russell, a merchant burgess, in the 16th century and was briefly occupied by Oliver Cromwell in the 17th.

certainly, it gave shelter for a night to Oliver Cromwell whose army was drawn up nearby.

The authentic records, says John Geddie, only 'prove that it was built by Mungo Russell, City Treasurer.' The date 1582 (much too late for Mary to have been here as she was by then a prisoner in England), and his initials, M.R., may account for the Mary, Queen of Scots association that still clings, with the tenacity of an oft-repeated tale, to the old building. As the initials of his wife, Kitty Fisher, appear also, it seems unlikely that M.R. refers to Mary. Mungo Russell was the owner of the adjacent Dalry Mills where he continued the manufacture of paper which had been started here by his German predecessor, Dalry having been one of the first paper mills in the Edinburgh area. He had bought the land in 1576.

Roseburn House, now in close proximity to Murrayfield Rugby ground, was enlarged in the 17th century and is still in private ownership. THE MILL HOUSE next door is now an Abbeyfield House.

West of Coltbridge on the south side of Corstorphine Road is MURRAYBANK, formerly the farmhouse of the Roseburn House home farm.

Slateford

Very little now remains of the village of Slateford. It grew up, in the parish of Colinton, around a crossing point on the Water of Leith, and the name is derived from the ford and the slaty character of the local stone. SLATEFORD HOUSE, built in the second half of the 18th century, is on the west side of the river in Lanark Road opposite Inglis Green Road and has a gabled and turreted southern extension.

At the back of Slateford House is the former Slateford Secession Church. Originally built in 1785, the church was radically altered in the early 19th century. The former manse is at No. 45 Lanark Road. Known as THE OLD MANSE, it is a two-storeyed house with two large attic dormer windows. It stands among trees beside the river on which it has fishing rights. The Secession Church was approached latterly through the late-Victorian stone gateway which, with its battlemented archway, still survives just short of

Slateford House, as does, a little further north in Lanark Road, CRAIGLOCKHART LODGE (see Craiglockhart House).

Spylaw Farm, or
Upper Spylaw Mill, House

Across Spylaw Public Park and westward a short distance along the footpath by the Water of Leith lies the old rubble-built house with the typically Scottish feature of a large chimney stack above the centre of the main frontage that is known as Spylaw Farm, or Upper Spylaw

Spylaw Farmhouse, or Upper Spylaw, stands by the Water of Leith and was once a smugglers' inn.

Mill, House. An attic window has been inserted into the lower part of the chimney masonry and the other chimneys are on the gables.

One of the earliest mills on the river was operated here. In 1590 permission was granted by the Privy Council to a German emigrant to manufacture paper in Scotland, without competition, for a period of nine years. It was none too successful to begin with, but it is known that paper was being made here as late as 1682. In the first quarter of the 18th century Upper Spylaw was converted to a snuff mill, with the top floor being used as an inn which is reputed to have been much frequented by smugglers.

At the end of the 18th century seventy-one mills, including flour, snuff, paper and timber mills, were located along the banks of the Water of Leith.

Spylaw House

The name of James Gillespie is inseparably associated with Spylaw House standing hard by the Water of Leith in the deep valley below Colinton Village. He and his younger brother John were tobacco merchants with a shop in the High Street of Edinburgh. James owned several snuff mills on the banks of the river, and the mill where he lived was the one at Spylaw, the mill being behind and beneath the house. The original house was built in 1650 but a northern Georgian addition (providing a new frontage) with a central pedimented feature was made in 1773. The building has two storeys and a basement with an iron balcony on the 18th century facade.

When James died in 1797 in his eightieth year he was a man of considerable wealth and, being unmarried, his estate was bequeathed in the interests of a charitable foundation. Governors were appointed and in 1801 a royal charter enabled them to proceed to the erection of James Gillespie's Hospital and Free School. The first persons admitted to the Hospital were to be Gillespie's own servants and then all men and women over fifty-five who bore his name. If there were still room within the institution anyone of that age in Edinburgh and Leith, failing which from other places in Midlothian, was to be deemed eligible. It was built near Tollcross (where the snuff merchant has given his name to Gillespie Crescent) in 1803, but in 1870 the foundation was changed to allow it to become a primary school, the elderly occupants being given pensions of about £20 a year. This building was demolished in 1976 but, as it was in a style derisively referred to as 'Carpenter's Gothic', it may well have been expendable!

James Gillespie was buried in Colinton Churchyard and his house, the grounds of which have for long been a public park, has been converted into flats after serving as a Scout Headquarters for a number of years.

Stenhouse Mansion

Stenhouse Mansion, or Stenhopemill, on the west bank of the Water of Leith near Gorgie, takes its name from the ancient Stenhope family and dates mainly from 1623. It has been said that it looked like the stranded hulk of 'some battered and decayed

Stenhouse Mansion, built largely in 1623, is now in the ownership of The National Trust for Scotland.

three-decker – a waif out of the early seventeenth century on which man's hand has fallen still more heavily than that of time' and its fabric has indeed had to be rescued more than once. On account of its age and its great interest, however, it has been well worth the efforts to conserve it.

The Stenhopes had been a merchant family and it was a merchant burgess and Treasurer of the city, Patrick Ellis (or Eleis) who added a three-storey wing in the centre of the north side and a two-storey extension to the south. Over the door and now re-painted in heraldic colours is a shield charged with a sword between two helmets with the initials P.E., the date 1623 and the motto 'Blisit. Be. God. For. Al. His. Giftis'. The words of an early Reformation 'grace before meat', they were often 'carvit in stane aboon their doors at hame'. The whole house has an appearance of antiquity, enhanced by steeply pitched roofs, crowstepped gables supporting massive chimney stacks, dormer windows with little pediments and finials and a feature once familiar in Edinburgh as elsewhere at a time when glass was scarce and expensive, windows with fixed glazing above and wooden shutters, which could be opened to admit fresh air, beneath. An unusual 'amenity' discovered in the gable basement walls consists of two triangular 'hen holes' with sixteen laying boxes behind them in the wall, hen-coops being much less common in buildings of this age than the more numerous pigeon lofts.

By the end of the 19th century the house had deteriorated to slum conditions, the rooms being sub-divided and let to labourers. In 1938, however, it was presented to The National Trust for Scotland by the Greyhound Racing Association, when a fine decorated ceiling was uncovered in the King Charles Room, after the removal of plaster, with the royal insignia and the date 1661. Conservation work was interrupted by the Second World War and the building was found to have fallen again into disrepair during these years and the ceiling to have been badly damaged by vandals. A rescue operation was once more mounted and this fine old house is now in use as a conservation centre.

SAUGHTON MILL COTTAGE, stone-built, slate-roofed and now divided into two separate dwellinghouses with neat front gardens, stands nearby in Stenhouse Mill Lane.

Struan Lodge

At the western end of Balgreen Avenue stands, within its garden and on the edge of Carrick Knowe Golf Course, the Victorian house called Struan Lodge but originally known as Saughton Vale. A niece of Earl Haig, Madame Gabrielle Dupree, removed to this house after the mansion of Saughtonhall in Gorgie Road was damaged by fire. In 1952, the building being too ruinous to be saved, it was deliberately destroyed by the Fire Brigade. (*Picturesque Notes of an Edinburgh Suburb: Coltbridge, Murrayfield, Roseburn.*) Between 1905 and 1914 the grounds had been laid out as Saughton Park and Rose Garden.

Waverley House

They come as a boon and a blessing to men,
The Pickwick, the Owl and the Waverley pen.

The name of the Victorian suburban house, in an architectural style which is something of an acquired taste, at No. 82 Colinton Road, was no doubt dictated by the occupation of its builder and recalls the little jingle that was once familiar well beyond the confines of Edinburgh. The Cameron family business of paper manufacture began in 1770 in Balerno but evolved into penmaking and the production of stationery with premises in Blair Street where the firm operated for over two hundred years and where their enamel signs can still be seen today. Fame was achieved by their ubiquitous pen nibs, the pens' users including such illustrious names as R.L. Stevenson, Gladstone and Rudyard Kipling.

Sir James Gowans (1822–90) (see Lammerburn), an architect whose work is enjoying a revival of interest, was commissioned by Duncan Cameron in 1884 to build the large family house at Craiglockhart which has long since ceased to be occupied by any member of the Cameron dynasty and which is now sub-divided. In line with the typical Gowans style, ornamental chimneys and gables are piled above plain and unpretentious walls, giving a top-heavy

Waverley House, at Craiglockhart, in 1985. It was built for a pen nib manufacturer by Sir James Gowans in 1884.

appearance to the building. The chimneys themselves are shaped like pen nibs around their tops.

At the end of the 19th century another jingle could be read in a shop window in the St. Leonards district of the city, but it was never as well known or as often quoted as the original couplet:

> Another pen, too, in the shape of a trowel
> Is equally good and its name is The Owl.
> A very queer name for a pen we must own,
> But if by its title 'tis meant to be shown
> That writers nocturnal are sounding its fame
> Then doubtless The Owl is the right sort of name.

Woodhall House

The 17th century Woodhall House can be found, isolated in a rural setting, at the western end of Woodhall Road at Colinton. The lands of Woodhall appear in the records as far back as 1329 and it was Adam Cunningham, Lord Woodhall, who, about 1630, built the house. Battlements and other neo-Gothic features were added in the early years of the 19th century. This seemly house is not enhanced by the modern, overpowering and incongruous block on the eastern side which has been converted into flats.

On the other side of the Water of Leith, the L-plan dwellinghouse behind the wall at No. 547 Lanark Road, the chimneys placed above the gables, was built as the WOODHALL DOWER HOUSE in the 18th century. It became St. Margaret's Manse when the church of

The isolated Woodhall House at Colinton was built for Lord Woodhall in the 17th century.

that name was erected in 1895. The church was demolished in 1978 when the manse became a private house.

CASTLEBANK, No. 500 Lanark Road at Juniper Green, conceals a small two-storeyed Georgian villa behind an austere battlemented frontage. A somewhat unusual house, it is described in *Buildings of Scotland: Edinburgh* as 'a castellated Gothic box' and certainly adds interest and variety to its surroundings.

Bibliography

Biographical Sketches and Illustrative Anecdotes to John Kay's Original Portraits and Caricature Etchings, 1837

The Buildings of Scotland: Edinburgh, 1984

Baillie, Simon J. *The Private World of Cammo*, 1995

Cant, Malcolm *Marchmont in Edinburgh*, 1984

Villages of Edinburgh, Vol. I, 1986

Chambers, Robert *Traditions of Edinburgh*, New Edition, 1868

Cockburn, Henry *Memorials of His Time*, 1856

Colvin, Howard *A Biographical Dictionary of British Architects 1600–1840*, 1978

Corstorphine Trust, The *Corstorphine Notes*, 1975

Cruickshank, W.G. *Duddingston Kirk and Village*, 1981

Easton, Drew, ed. *By the Three Great Roads: A History of Tollcross, Fountainbridge and the West Port*, 1988

Ferenbach, The Rev. Campbell *Annals of Liberton*, 1975

Fleming, John *Scottish Country Houses and Gardens Open to the Public*, 1954

Geddie, John *Romantic Edinburgh*, 1921

The Fringes of Edinburgh, n.d.

Good, George *Liberton in Ancient and Modern Times*, 1893

Grant, James *Old and New Edinburgh*, 1882

Gray, John G. *The South Side Story*, 1962

Gray, John G. and Smith, Charles J. *A Walk on the Southside in the Footsteps of Robert Burns*, 1998

Hanna, Dr William *Memoirs of Dr Chalmers*

Hannah, Ian C. *Triumphant Classicism* in *The Stones of Scotland*, ed. George Scott-Moncrieff, 1938

Harrison, Wilmot *Memorable Edinburgh Houses*, 1893, republished 1971

Hunter, R.L. *Trinity Grove: The Story of an Old Edinburgh House*, n.d.

Inglis, Francis Caird *The Barony of Calton and District*, 1936

Mackay, John *History of the Barony of Broughton*, 1869

Mackenzie-Stuart, A.J. *A French King at Holyrood*, 1995

Mair, William *Historic Morningside*, 1947

Marshall, The Rev. Dr James Scott *The Life and Times of Leith*, 1986

Mitchell, Ann *The People of Calton Hill*, 1993

Peterkin, G.A.G. *Scottish Dovecotes*, 1980

Picturesque Notes of an Edinburgh Suburb: Coltbridge, Murrayfield, Roseburn, n.d., The Murrayfield Residents' Association

Pipes, Rosemary J. *The Colonies of Stockbridge*, 1984

Pope Hennessy, James *Robert Louis Stevenson*, 1974

Russell, John *The Story of Leith*, 1922

Simpson, Eve Blantyre *The R.L. Stevenson Originals*, 1912

Skinner, Basil C. *The House on the Bridge*, 1982

Smart, Alastair *The Life and Art of Allan Ramsay*, 1952

Smith, Charles J. *Historic South Edinburgh*, 1979
Morningside, 1992

Smith, Donald *John Knox House*, 1996.

Smith, John *Dalry House: Its Lands and Owners* in *The Book of the Old Edinburgh Club*, Vol. XX, 1935

Steuart, James *Notes for a History of Colinton Parish*, 1938

Stevenson, Robert Louis *Edinburgh: Picturesque Notes*, 1897

Wallace, Joyce M. *Great King Street and the Second New Town of Edinburgh* 1972
Traditions of Trinity and Leith, Second Edition, 1997

Wood, Marguerite *Edinburgh Castle*, HMSO, 1953

Youngson, A.J. *The Making of Classical Edinburgh*, 1966

Index
1. Houses

Index

2. People

Index

Index